BE THAT AS IT MAY!

or

Ten Stupid Things

Governments do to Mess Up

Edyucaishun

By Roberta Maclise McDonald

(With acknowledgement to
Harper Collins for use of similar title)

Order this book online at www.trafford.com/07-1634
or email orders@trafford.com

Most Trafford titles are also available at major online book retailers.

© Copyright 2007 Roberta Maclise McDonald.
Cover Design or Artwork by Peter E. McDonald.
All rights reserved. No part of this publication may be reproduced, stored in a retrieval system, or transmitted, in any form or by any means, electronic, mechanical, photocopying, recording, or otherwise, without the written prior permission of the author.

Note for Librarians: A cataloguing record for this book is available from Library and Archives Canada at www.collectionscanada.ca/amicus/index-e.html

Printed in Victoria, BC, Canada.

ISBN: 978-1-4251-4016-8

We at Trafford believe that it is the responsibility of us all, as both individuals and corporations, to make choices that are environmentally and socially sound. You, in turn, are supporting this responsible conduct each time you purchase a Trafford book, or make use of our publishing services. To find out how you are helping, please visit www.trafford.com/responsiblepublishing.html

Our mission is to efficiently provide the world's finest, most comprehensive book publishing service, enabling every author to experience success. To find out how to publish your book, your way, and have it available worldwide, visit us online at www.trafford.com/10510

www.trafford.com

North America & international
toll-free: 1 888 232 4444 (USA & Canada)
phone: 250 383 6864 ♦ fax: 250 383 6804
email: info@trafford.com

The United Kingdom & Europe
phone: +44 (0)1865 722 113 ♦ local rate: 0845 230 9601
facsimile: +44 (0)1865 722 868 ♦ email: info.uk@trafford.com

10 9 8 7 6 5 4 3 2

DEDICATION

This book is dedicated to my grandchildren – Jade, Macey, and Reagan – as well as all future children - in hopes they will have rich and rewarding learning experiences and grow up with open minds, the knowledge to back up what they say, and the courage to stand up for what they think is morally right.

ACKNOWLEDGEMENTS

With gratitude to my husband, Peter, for his art work and for letting me use him as a sounding board for many of the ideas in this book. I also acknowledge and thank my children, Megan and Justin, who helped with the computer "newspeak" which becomes complicated from the tenth word onwards. Moreover, they and all my past students must be given credit for affording me the opportunity to experience life in school through their eyes. Children are much too honest to hide how they feel as they go through life's trials and tribulations. They constantly remind adults that without them there is no future. For this insight, we must be mindful and careful as to what we pass on to them.

TABLE OF CONTENTS

	TITLE	PAGE NO.
Introduction	Be That as it May	3
Chapter I	Academic Misdirections	11
Chapter II	Top Down Administration	23
Chapter III	Mandatory Unions	40
Chapter IV	Time and Money Wasters	55
Chapter V	Low Public Accountability	73
Chapter VI	Pressure Groups	90
Chapter VII	Dress Code	110
Chapter VIII	Back to Basics	120
Chapter IX	Democratizing Disciplines	134
Chapter X	Safety is Killing Physical Exercise	145
Epilogue	Recommendations for the Future	156

INTRODUCTION: BE THAT AS IT MAY

"The unexamined life is not fit to be lived, "

Socrates (2400 years ago)

Therefore, I examine my life in trying to make sense of what has happened in as objective a manner as possible. Naturally, that is an impossible task seeing as I am speaking of my own life, from my own perspective. However, I shall try. Hopefully, others will see fit to read these words and find a corner of their lives which may be viewed in a different light. A dialectic will begin, even if only in their own minds. I know that my life has been affected greatly by words that others have written or spoken. This is my attempt to pass on things I have learned through life experience.

This book will be written in plain language, often in point form because my objective for doing this is to make it easy for parents and other interested persons to peruse quickly. So much more is expected of parents in today's society, in terms of family responsibilities. Maybe that is why many young couples have decided against having children. The average family with children experiences a rather chaotic life trying to juggle full-time jobs plus all the expectations regarding children such as involving them in sports or the arts, fund-raising and organizations for these activities, social and schooling demands, safety precautions, etcetera; so that they have little time to read large, erudite tomes. They need short, explicit information to answer their education questions and suggest appropriate solutions in time to help with educating their children. The time is short and, as soon as your children are finished school, it is understandable that parents' interest in public education wanes quickly.

Whatever virtue there was originally in the public school's objectives it seems to have become an instrument for left wing goals in general philosophy and direction. These objectives lead to heavily centralized and regulated lifestyle choices. A letter to the editor by Paul Gordon of Ontario in 2003 expressed it quite well. "All are given the same education and culture in order that they sound the same and think the same: 'like a vegan, feminist, gay-activist, union-supporting, liberal ecologist." (*Calgary Herald*, 2003) It is time we, as parents, taxpayers, and citizens, take back control of the education of our children because (1) they are our children and not the state's and (2) we must attempt to raise open-minded children and informed citizens for the continuation of a civilized society whose minds are free to think and express their own thoughts. A mindset such as this should lead its graduates to pursue goals unfettered by dogma imposed from government or other overarching authority, no matter how benevolent that authority claims to be.

The opinions expressed herein spring from the perspective of my 46 years in and out of the classroom. I started teaching in 1959 and did my last stint of substitute teaching in 2005. During that time I finished three degrees, two undergraduate degrees, the first in Education, the second in general academic Arts & Science and, finally, one in post-graduate Education. Without any special plan for a career in the beginning I spent considerable time pursuing other goals besides Education ... in Real Estate, in Tax Preparation and other Accounting, in Horticulture, and in the Travel industry to name several. I include this information to show that I have some experience in other fields as well as education, and therefore am able to make some comparisons between public service and private business. My interest in Education became more acute after my own two children were in school, which is probably when most parents suddenly cue in to its special relevance. I had already taught for seven years when this happened and was becoming concerned about many of the things that were happening in the classroom. Official policies for Education were showing some strange directions in my opinion, but, had I not had children of my own, I probably would have dismissed these ideas and gone on to another type of work.

I returned to teaching when my youngest child entered kindergarten. As things turned out, due to provincial economics re: the National Energy Program, my own antipathy towards wrong-headed administrative directions, and most probably other personality factors, most of the rest of my teaching career was spent as a substitute teacher in the Calgary public schools with a few stints in other jurisdictions. There was even a short stint when I substituted for the Separate School system as well. Then I was informed that they were hiring only Catholics. Consequently, I was taken off their roster. It always seemed unfair to me that teachers of the Catholic persuasion could teach in the Public System, but not vice versa. However, that was definitely **NOT** a hill I wanted to die on. Besides there were many other issues of much more importance crowding my life.

As many of you are aware, the role of a substitute teacher is one of very low respect, and commensurate pay. For most of those years the extra benefits regular teachers enjoyed were non-existent for substitutes. Fortunately, my husband's union-benefits package covered me and the children for medical insurance. However, this low-rewards career path did afford me special insight into what was going on in hundreds of classrooms and with many different students.

My first teaching experience was in Regina, Saskatchewan, first in Grade One, then in Grades Two, Three, Four and Five. I then returned to university to finish my first degree. At that time teacher accreditation consisted of only one year of Teachers' College with another year-equivalent, which could be acquired through summer and winter classes. I continued by teaching Senior High English and Physical Education in Saskatoon, Saskatchewan. Next, I moved to Calgary and taught at the Junior High level. Later, I returned to my home in rural Saskatchewan because of family reasons and taught in Senior and Junior High, English, Social Studies, Health Education, Physical Education and Biology. Teaching in a small, rural community necessated being able to handle a broad range of academic subjects. Generally, I was a free spirit roaming around tasting life and enjoying the experiences.

Meanwhile, my mind was seriously thinking about the basic questions of Life. Where are we heading? How should we get there? What has History taught us about proper conduct, and ultimately good government policy? In other words, I had acquired an interest in politics and government. I decided to return to university to take an Arts degree and ponder the true academic aspects of learning. I consider that was the turning point in my life on the way to Socrates' ideal.

Marriage and children then came along interrupting my self-absorbed and vagrant way of life. However, both my husband and I have been curious about different places and experiences moving from Saskatchewan to Victoria, British Columbia, then back to Saskatchewan and finally to Alberta. In all of these places I have taught for mostly short periods of time in all levels from Kindergarten to Grade 12. I can truthfully say that rarely have I taught the same lesson more than once, scarcely a way to hone a master lesson or a full year course. However, I did become a master at innovation as well as coming up with lessons related to a wide variety of subjects in a quick hurry. I do not promote this way of life for everyone, certainly not as a profitable way of life. However, it has afforded me a good overview of what is going on in the classrooms of these three provinces. Here is my attempt to pass on this information and classroom experience to interested parents and the general public.

Education differs from many services in the following ways:

1. Most of the mistakes that are made take years to show the effects, so that the person or persons responsible need have little fear of having to pay directly in any way except perhaps for some personal angst.
2. Many of the objectives of education are intrinsic, that is, cannot be overtly tested or even vocalized truthfully. In other words, it becomes easy for someone to fake having learned some of the important lessons such as honesty, fairness, objectivity, and dedication.
3. Several of the subjects taught have no immediate relevance to the student; subjects such, but not limited to them: History, Literature, second or third languages, higher Mathematics, Advanced Sciences, civic responsibility, and love of learning itself.
4. Educators must recognize that many, if most children and even adults will never get to the stage of loving learning for its own sake. For these people, the value of learning something is measured in how it improves their lives economically and possibly, socially. John Gatto, a teacher for 35 years in the New York City schools has postulated that the basics of education, that is, literacy and numeracy, can be taught in about 100 hours of instruction PROVIDED THAT THEY ARE INTERESTED AND FOCUSED. (Gatto, John; *Dumbing Us Down*, 1992) Our school systems insist children stay in school until they are 15 years old, in most cases, far more than is necessary to accomplish the primary goal. Many problems arise from our unwillingness to question this postulate.
5. Bureaucracies are generally unresponsive to recommendations unless forced to pay attention by huge consequences that refuse to be ignored. Example: in the Justice System, the policy of soft on crime finally resulted in the unnecessary deaths of four policemen before a big overhaul of the RCMP hierarchy was undertaken. Although this is an extreme example, it relates directly to what has become the norm for much classroom behavior and will be dealt with in Chapter Two.

6. Education has become a huge cost factor for the public domain. It now accounts for at least 25% of provincial budgets, which have the mandate to provide it. This does not mean the federal and municipal governments are excluded. Besides being responsible for aboriginal educational funding, education has become a major plank in recent Federal government election platforms. Municipal governments, too, have weighed in on these issues through lobbying and taxation levies. The public should therefore be keenly interested in what is happening since it affects them so directly every day of their working lives.

7. Education is a "feel good " area of interest, like motherhood and apple pie   USED to be. Many politicians are expressing their extreme interest in education as well as adopting the stance that more and more money is needed to solve the problem. These solutions, in my opinion, stem from either a false interest, a means to make themselves look good, or a poor understanding of how to improve some obvious limitations and failings of the system.

As you read these words, you will probably ask yourself, "Everything seems to be wrong with our education system. How can that be? How does it happen that reports keep coming out saying how wonderful it is?" I want you to examine the source of those reports. They are mostly self-congratulatory as is an advertisement from any business. Does that mean we should blindly accept their personal boasting? Of course not. We need some outside, objective evaluations, plus observation and evaluation of long-term results from OUTSIDE the system.

Many studies have been done, but they are generally dull reading as well as grade and subject specific. Very few of us are motivated to go through the tedious work of reading them. We leave it to the media to evaluate these for us, not realizing that the major media sources are part of the establishment that likes it this way. This situation keeps them in that special hallowed position, as interpreters of what is good. I will try to cite some of these major studies and help you make sense of them.

Long-term results are topics of general interest, mostly in the "Imagine that!" category. For example, " My new employee cannot make change without a calculator or a cash register. Imagine that!" Business responded to that deficiency by developing bar codes and installing laser readers so cashiers no longer need that skill in their jobs. Although those innovations solved an immediate problem for business, they did not really address the underlying problem. In our personal lives, we feel ashamed if we cannot succeed at simple mental tasks. We tend to hide our deficiencies in a multitude of ways. That is okay in the short run, but unacceptable for those of us who have spent years getting educated as well as for the general public who realize, too late, their acumen of mental skills and knowledge are severely lacking. The paper diplomas and degrees we hold are, sadly, worth little in fact.

So the problems have remained hidden for years as the costs go up. Not least of these costs include the negative effects it has on our children. In my experience, over half the students were turned off by the middle school years, warming seats in school, but learning very little. In my adult life, I have met many mature adults who have a mediocre education at best, content to fill their mental lives with mindless entertainments eagerly swallowing the half truths, distortions, and lies that we are being fed day after day. Moreover, our world has suddenly turned dangerous both in general philosophy and militarily which makes the role of teaching and learning that much more critical in our global community. It is crucial that we have a clear understanding of what is going on around us.

Getting a good education remains one of our most fundamental goals, as well it should. To deny your mind the critical thinking skills it needs in order to make sense of life may have been good enough for the barbaric life of the Dark Ages, but is totally unacceptable today.

CHAPTER ONE – ACADEMIC MISDIRECTIONS

"What better gift can we offer the country than to teach and instruct our youth?"

Cicero, 160-43 B.C.

In 1953 Hilda Neatby wrote a book called *So Little for the Mind* in which she argued that the newly-adopted progressive education model based on John Dewey's ideas were debasing the most worthwhile subjects. Dewey's ideas were being implemented all across United States and Canada as the new and enlightened methods of education. These methods included an entirely new way to teach English, giving rise to the Dick and Jane series of readers for Grades One to Three. History, Geography, Moral Ethics, and Civics were replaced with a subject called Social Studies. Logic and Rhetoric were completely thrown out being as outdated and unnecessary, ditto Latin.

Children chanted; "Latin is a dead language;
        Dead as dead can be.
        It killed the ancient Romans
        And now it's killing me."

I started my schooling in 1946 just as these progressive methods were being introduced into pioneer, outback Saskatchewan in a one-room schoolhouse housing Grades One to Nine. It is interesting to realize that these new ideas for education had already extended into such remote areas. Therefore, dear reader, you can comprehend how all-pervasive these ideas had become. In post-World War II and post-Depression era, the ideas of Socialism were taking hold all across the world, notwithstanding the fact that most of the immigrants had come to this country seeking more freedom and the right to own private property, ideas anathema to socialism one would think. However, these pioneers were extremely busy building a life for themselves, and very grateful that a benevolent government was going to educate their children for them. Public communications consisted mainly of a weekly newspaper and perhaps daily radio news broadcasts, if you were lucky enough to own a radio. In addition to the busy life in which most pioneers were engaged, most of my parents' friends and neighbors were barely literate or poorly educated themselves and did not have the background to appreciate what was going on in the venerated field of education. For example, both my maternal grandparents who lived with us at the end of their lives were completely illiterate. From what I understand of history, the public authorities in Ukraine did not think it was necessary for simple peasants to get an education. In fact, keeping them ignorant made it easier to control them. Through it all, though, they held onto the idea that education was very important making sure that all of their children went to school. In retrospect, it is understandable that few objected to these new directions at that time.

This watershed in the field of education occurred at the time when Tommy Douglas was the Premier of Saskatchewan, the same Tommy Douglas who is credited with starting our hallowed public health care system; the same one who was voted the most important Canadian of the Twentieth Century by the Canadian Broadcasting Corporation in 2004. Canada had taken a huge Left turn. That direction has continued more or less unabated until today in most parts of Canada, despite the failures, excesses, and enormous atrocities committed in its name around the world. To be fair, most of these atrocities were yet unknown. The Soviet Union and its apologists in the Free World had done a masterful job of covering up such things as the starvation of eight million Ukrainians in their rush to collectivize the farms. Rumours of mass starvation, incidentally, were investigated by the *New York Times*, which sent an expeditionary news team there at this time. They came back with the news that these rumours were false, an assertion that finally was recanted in 2003. If facts of this magnitude could be covered up, how easy it was for lesser evils to be glossed over or spun to give advantage to so-called "progressive" policies.

Education became the flagship of this new movement. People must be re-educated in order to be "open" to these new ideas. Gradually, provincial governments and local School Boards adopted all of these new, progressive methods as well as the new subjects that were needed for the "brave new world" described by George Orwell in his book of the same name.

I really don't know the full extent of studies which Dewey carried out in order to test these ideas, but I doubt they were comprehensive in any way. I do know that his ideas were more philosophical than empirical, and very pervasive in my teacher training courses, 1958 to 1963. Any questions or arguments countering or questioning the veracity of these ideas were played down at best; more frequently they were treated as naïve, ignorant arguments offered by unsophisticated people from the backwoods. A friend of mine recounted an experience in university where an older student, disgusted by the Keynesian theories of economics, slammed down his books and walked out rather than have to swallow more of these theories he considered wrong-headed and untested. His arguments in class to this effect had been met with consistent ridicule. The fact that none of the rest of the students, many of him harboring the same thoughts, did not follow his example is a testament to how timid most of us are.

The following is a partial list of some of these directions, or should I say, mis-directions for education:

1. Repetitive exercises, including rote learning, is the lowest form of learning. Stay away from it.
2. No more dull mathematics or spelling drills, geography games, or spelling bees.
3. Competitive games teach children to be combative rather than cooperative and therefore should be discouraged.
4. Memorizing poems, dates, or any information is a poor way to enhance learning.
5. Reading out loud is an outdated method of testing students' ability to read and, furthermore humiliates those students who read poorly.
6. Students should not be seated in rows and forced to work on their own.
7. Design classroom seating arrangements any way except in rows facing the teacher; perhaps around tables, in circles, even with backs to the teacher.
8. Group work is preferable to individual seatwork.
9. A good teacher doesn't teach out of textbooks or for the test. A true professional strives for lessons which are imaginative and innovative.
10. No child shall be forced to stand in order to answer a question. In fact, no child shall be forced to answer, period. This may disturb his/her self-esteem.
11. Teachers must be constantly sensitive to a child's self-esteem so as not to damage it. In essence, it became a sacred cow in education. Leading educators even hinted that the real reason students cannot learn is because of lack of self-esteem, a favorite theme of several daytime talk shows.
12. School Boards should adopt a "No fail" policy because failure stigmatizes students.
13. Keep students of the same age and size together despite their varying academic abilities. Institute remedial courses and a Spiral curriculum to patch up any missing information or academic skills.
14. Many students are non-academic, therefore you must develop special courses for them, properly dumbed-down so that they can relate.

15. Mastery of the Basics must take a back seat to the principles of self-esteem. Students will be able to pick up skills and information missed in earlier grades (another reason for the Spiral Curriculum).
16. Teachers should be facilitators rather than lecturers or directors of learning. Direct instruction from a teacher means he/she is a poor/mediocre teacher and will be graded as such.
17. Subjects should be geared to students' interests, perhaps by asking them what they wish to learn. Do not limit your teaching to the old-fashioned disciplines for subject matter. Movies such as "To Sir, with Love" reinforced this idea.
18. One of a teacher's main jobs is to "motivate" students, by whatever means necessary. If a student shows a disincentive to learn it is because the teacher has not shown enough initiative in engaging him or her.
19. Schools should be constructed with open areas and without lofty roofs or big windows so as not to intimidate students or make them feel inadequate. In fact, windows are largely distracting to concentration as well as unnecessary now that we have modern electric lighting.

Quite a list! Not complete by any stretch, either, and definitely a new wrinkle on twinkle. Were they necessary? Had the old methods failed so badly? New inventions and conveniences were being introduced every year and people's lives, even in outback Saskatchewan, were gradually becoming easier and more enjoyable. So why did we need a complete change of direction? Maybe these ideas bore examining more closely. At the very least perhaps we should go slow, and with caution, re-evaluating at every step.

Along came the very person for the job in the person of Ms. Neatby. She was well-educated, a realist and, most important, a local resident. Most of these ideas had been generated in United States, our nearest neighbor which was much more developed and urban that rural Western Canada. Maybe these methods and ideas were okay for them, but not for us. Any farmer's daughter or son who suffered through Dick and Jane's urban lifestyle books knows how foreign to us was the life depicted in this series.

Neatby's book was a revelation to me. I was an undergraduate at the University of Saskatchewan, Saskatoon, where Ms. Neatby had taught for years. At the time I held little interested in politics or economics, or education for that matter, besides being VERY short of money. (For those of you interested in economics, my sister and I prided ourselves on completing one year of university with a total of $800.00 each.) Nevertheless, her book intrigued me to the extent that it was one of the few books that I purchased other than textbooks. How right she was, as time has proven. However, have any of her reservations and analyses been taken seriously enough to re-evaluate the public education system? Not to my knowledge and experiences in the field. Changes have been made, but mostly the changes made have consisted of going further down the same path, always with the excuse that if these methods and courses are not succeeding it is because of lack of dollars. How discouraging when you consider that generations of young people have been crippled academically because of them.

As well, it is interesting to note that she published the book while she was a professor, and she continued in her profession until retirement. In today's university climates, she may have been fired for hate literature, or dismissed as an "extremist". Forty-seven years later Dr. Diane Ravitch echoed the conclusions of Neatby in her book published in New York entitled, *Left Back: A Century of Failed School Reforms*. I can already hear the apologists for official progressive education saying, "That only pertains to the Americans. Everybody knows their system sucks." Weird, because John Dewey was also an American, the very one who engineered the whole system. Ravitch also revealed that this system had its beginning in the 1920's in United States. By the later 1940's many of its shortcomings were already becoming evident. Despite these looming questions, Canada was ready to plunge ahead. It seems the worst and slowest learners are the education professors.

Now let us examine the problems with some of these new directions as they pertained to my experience:

1. Memorization is good for the brain. And the best time in life to memorize anything is when you are young. Children's minds are like sponges up to the age of their teens. This is evident if you have had the good fortune to have grandchildren close around. There is some evidence to suggest that you can "grow" a brain by lots of memorization. Understanding comes later.

2. Spelling Bees have come back with a vengeance in the last few years, perhaps as a result of it becoming common knowledge that few graduates could spell any longer. Spell Check programs on the computer failed to solve all the problems because English (and most languages) have so many homonyms and abbreviations that can only be corrected by knowledge of spelling rules. Geography has not yet made a comeback. I'm still hopeful.

3. As for competitions, any teacher can tell you the easiest way to motivate students is with a competitive game. "Boys against girls" will perk up the ears and energies of any child ... adult, too, for that matter. Why cut out a natural part of our human psyches? Actually, it can't be done. When the school refuses to institute any and all competitions, students will invent their own games, such as, who is wearing the most "cool" clothes? Who has the most friends? Who is the biggest class clown? You get the idea.

4. If memorizing poems is so bad for you, how come young people walk around with their ears plugged into pop songs? They live by the words of some of these songs. Many teenagers hardly know the words to old, familiar folksongs yet they can repeat the lyrics of many of the advertisements from television.

5. Reading out loud is a quick and easy way to tell how well a child has learned to read, a fundamental skill for any subject. The sooner you do this the better, since it becomes more and more embarrassing for a child as s/he gets older.

6. Row seating makes the best arrangement for large classes. They can see the teacher and the chalkboard, overhead projector, the poster, etc. plus she/he can see their faces which are the mirrors of the mind. By reading faces the teacher usually can tell whether the students understand the concepts without resorting to tests or seatwork. Whenever the students do get to have another seating arrangement, it becomes a special event. Children, especially young children, thrive in an atmosphere that is predictable and orderly.

7. I have been in a hundred classroom where children are seated in little "chat groups", very conducive to socializing, but hardly effective for concentrating on academics. These groupings are meant to facilitate group work, which is problematic at any level, and one big problem for elementary and even senior grades as they constantly bicker over whose pencil, eraser, crayon, etc. is whose. Why, I wonder, do we as adults sit in chairs facing the podium where we politely listen to the speaker if learning is better done by turning your back on him/her? I guess adults are too backward to learn these "new" techniques. Classrooms have become mazes for teachers to traverse as they detour around scattered desks, haphazard arrangements of chairs, and backpacks littered on the floor.

8. Group work is based on the principle that the workplace is generally occupied by more than one person. Therefore, children should learn to work in groups since this better emulates the work place. Teach them how to be a "team player." Only teachers it seems can be fooled by such specious logic. Learning is much different from a workplace. Producing a product often requires the talents of several people whereas it is impossible to learn much by absorbing it through someone else's effort. Nine times out of ten, two students do the work, the others chat. Then everyone gets

the same mark. Those who do the work feel cheated and used; those who have done little if anything may feel guilty, but do not hesitate to take advantage of it. Group work has its uses, but should be limited to specific projects that lend themselves to that format.

9. Not teaching for the test is one of the most idiotic ideas yet that has come out of progressive education. What if a manufacturer kept his workers gainfully employed, but did not insist that they made a good product? What if an engineer built a thirty-storey skyscraper, but did not test his concrete or steel products to make sure they didn't collapse from the first wind? Naturally you want your students not only to pass the test, but to do so with flying colors. That is not to say that every word that is uttered is directly related to the upcoming test (as if anyone knows everything that was or is going to be on it), but generally, the material you cover in class should be relevant to what you are going to test them on. How elementary! How sensible! But I forgot we buried Common Sense along with our ideas of Hypocrisy a couple of generations ago.

10. Standing to answer a question or to count the Roster went out even before I entered school. I guess it embarrassed shy people so much they refused to come to school. However, the idea of catering to students who do not want to answer anything orally has gone too far. It makes the learning atmosphere in a classroom impossible for the teacher in many cases. Therefore many classes are conducted by giving out worksheets where even senior students just fill in the blanks. However, it is true, having the right to say "No" to a teacher who asks you to stand and answer a question does increase the student's self-esteem which continues to be a major objective. That this behavior diminishes the teacher's position is not a consideration, apparently.

11. The same can be said for the "No Fail" policy... absolutely idiotic, but good for Self-Esteem. It is now acknowledged our graduates are more sure of themselves than they

have ever been in Canada's history.... At least until they get their first real job. The impetus for this policy swept the school system starting in the 1970's, incidentally at a time when I was at home with my children. When I returned to teaching in the early 1980's I was brought up to date with a jolt. A Grade Seven boy had failed the year before. He didn't care; he didn't like school and was waiting for his fifteenth birthday when he could leave school. Consequently, whenever a test was scheduled, he either made sure he was absent or barely attempted to write anything down. When I reminded him of the logical consequences (of failure, that is) he informed me he didn't care, as stated above. Otherwise he was a reasonably likeable child and presented no big problems in terms of behavior. At the end of the year, I made out his report card as required failing him in all subjects in which he had been my student. The principal then informed me of the new Board policy. This student could not fail and I must comply by giving him a passing grade. I refused. Not a good policy for teacher without tenure, a nirvana I never achieved. The upshot was that the principal revised the report card himself. I was appalled that a simple policy could override a realistic fact. My ignorance of how powerful these forces were and are has been a thorn in my side throughout my educational career, I hasten to add.

12. Being bigger and taller than the rest of the class can be embarrassing, certainly, but is not the worst thing a child can experience. Children that have passed from grade to grade without ever learning the minimum skills and knowledge either grow quieter and quieter, or conversely become the class clown and endeavor (often successfully in my experience) to interfere greatly in the learning and teaching for the rest of the class. The Spiral Curriculum has been a big failure as well. Soon reluctant students realize they really don't have to master anything academic because it will come up again later. Furthermore, students are not fooled by the lowering of standards in various courses. They know that "basket-weaving" is for the dummies, as is English 13, Math 14, et cetera. They laugh about it openly. Inwardly, that's a different story.

The major negative effect results in lack of mental development, so little for the mind, just as Dr. Neatby and others predicted and observed. This objective also has a negative on the good students who become bored with the repetitions.

13. Teachers as facilitators rather than directors of learning has proven to be a failure as well. Many studies have been conducted comparing the two basic methods with direct instruction from a teacher winning out hands down. Several of the Charter schools have re-instituted Direct Instruction, as have most of the successful Private Schools. Japan primarily uses this method showing overwhelmingly that successful learning is accomplished more easily and quickly.

14. I recall with ease the shock I experienced in Teachers' College when I heard our instructor say that students should be in charge of what they wished to learn. As a young person it then appealed to my sense of superiority (which most young people possess as a natural part of growing up). More sober reflection later on and out in the field made me change my mind. Common sense can tell you that **KNOWING WHAT YOU DON'T KNOW** is impossible. I don't deny that children, even young children, can come up with the most amazing questions. For example, my four-year-old granddaughter the other day mused at the table, "Why do adults like to sit and talk all the time?" So I don't discount that educators should listen to what children say and the questions they ask, but to have them decide what topics to pursue and how to approach them is nothing short of simple-minded. However, this misdirection espoused by top educators has been repeated many times throughout my teaching career. I suspect it might still be part of teacher training curricula.

15. Demanding that teachers motivate students to learn has left most teachers scratching their heads. I guess the obvious question is "Why?" Is not education and learning an important objective of most people's lives, second only to the more basic needs of security, shelter, and food? We should all be taking salesmanship training then. I must say I learned more about motivation from my training for a realtor than from

my teacher training. We need to re-examine this postulate very seriously, and, I hope, very soon.

16. Re-designing schools to accommodate new directions in education took on serious costs during the 1970's. "Open area" classrooms meant most of the present schools would not suffice, and were structurally impossible to modify. Architects and builders had a hey-day. After all, this was public money which often signifies a bottomless pit. Without going into detail, let me say that I have taught in several of these open area schools and found them very chaotic, more chaotic than even ordinary modern classrooms, which is not a mean trick. Very soon, within a couple of years in fact, temporary walls were being set up within these open areas. I think most of them have morphed into permanent walls once again. So much for open areas.

Some of the more recent themes and directions are even more contradictory, puzzling, and frightening.. One new paradigm in education seems to be that there are no Absolutes, everything is Relative, even Truth, according to one's culture and environment. For example, children brought up in ghettos cannot relate to middle class values. Children of immigrants must be allowed latitude when it comes to academic expectations, customs, dress, and a myriad list of other expectations, even language in many cases.

This development is labeled Moral and Social Relativism. The headaches from this newest paradigm are so recent as to be as yet undetermined. Many feel they may threaten or in fact undermine our whole country. That is a topic much too broad for this book, so I will leave it there. Maybe all these atrocities cannot be attributed to the public education system, but it must bear some of the blame. Who else controls our children's minds in their most vulnerable and impressionable years? The Catholic Church used to say, in essence, "Give me your son until he is fourteen years and I will have him for life." It sounds ominous. This book is my attempt to answer that challenge.

CHAPTER TWO: TOP-DOWN ADMINISTRATION

"The diploma gives society a phantom guarantee and its holders phantom rights."

Valery, 1871-1945.

No teacher in the classroom runs her/his own ship any longer. In other words, all decisions regarding class management are subject to the approval or disapproval of the administrators directly above them. In the distant past, i.e. when I was in elementary school, this practice was limited to the Area Superintendent who visited intermittently to review what was being taught, and if the students were concentrating on the curriculum. As students, we were unaware that our teacher was being evaluated as well. In our modern, mostly-city classrooms under the factory school system, the personnel involved could include (and often does) Department Heads (now usually called Subject Program Directors), Counselors, Assistant Principals, Principals, Area Assistant Superintendents, Main Superintendent, and the whole raft of provincial hierarchy up to the Minister of Education. That's a lot of bosses.

The justification for this model is based on the business model we are told. My question is, how can teaching in a compulsory public institution paid for out of the public purse be compared to a personal business which must (1) invest its/their own money, time, and talents (2) advertise or in other ways find its own clients, and (3) make a profit in order to survive? Many checks and balances exist in the business world including adherence to the laws and taxes of the land. The same conditions do not apply to the Public Education institution.

Teachers have been striving for years to become recognized as professionals, yet they seem to readily accept these restrictions on their professionalism. Other professionals do not; for example, doctors, lawyers, accountants, psychologists, dentists, architects, engineers, et cetera. All these groups must acquire certain training sanctioned by provincial or federal laws, which in turn, issues them a certificate, as in Education. The similarity ends there, however. Then, these professionals can either join an ongoing business or start one of their own. None of their clients (except now for the medical profession which is rapidly becoming a socialist quagmire) are forced to go to them. Therefore, why must teachers who have obtained their government sanctioned degrees and certificates then be forced to submit to the public school system in order to get clients? Why couldn't they put out a shingle advertising for clients/students, teach those subjects mandated by the Government Curriculum, submit these clients to basic tests or examinations by one Boss i.e. a government Superintendent or Minister. Their success would depend on their ability to attract clients/parents who would in turn entrust them with educating their children? These mavericks could get paid in the same way as now, based on what the government spends per child.

You might argue that a teacher can do just that, and several very brave souls have done so. However, no government largess is forthcoming without gargantuan efforts on the part of that individual or group of individuals. Public education funding continues to be a government policy where the money goes **ONLY** to government-sanctioned institutions. This policy has led to a completely Top-Down system with all its requisite problems and shortcomings.

Top-Down administration has had many negative results over the years in my opinion, not the least of these in the field of discipline. I doubt you could find many parents who have spent considerable time in a modern classroom who would vouch positively for the normal confusion that seems to reign there. I know apologists for public education would respond that this assessment is "Old-fashioned, outdated, rigid, undemocratic, maybe even racist and discriminatory." Many of these students come from "deprived" backgrounds and therefore need special treatment using multiple different "learning styles". If these reasons do not convince, the next postulate lays the blame completely at the feet of the parents. How, I wonder, can parents have such sterling control over their children to be able to know and insist on proper behavior in a school far from their immediate location?

The truth is that little academic learning is going on there. I still recall with some clarity and humiliation the incident that inspired the title of this book. It occurred in a Calgary junior high school specifically designated for Learning Disabled students. Expecting a tough day, I psyched myself up on the way to school promising myself to (1) not lose my temper (2) not raise my voice (3) be patient and non-demanding, but KEEP ORDER by clearly stated, simple rules of "One person at a time", and "Stay in your desks until the lesson is explained."

The bell had barely sounded when pushing, jostling students made it apparent that instituting these policies was not going to be easy. I waited for them to settle down a little. Five minutes later, some order seemed to ensue. Suddenly the door burst open and three girls entered in high dungeon screaming at each other over some disagreement. A minute later, one rushed up to me demanding to go out to the bathroom. I vainly tried to object whereupon she screamed at me, "I HAVE TO GO!" "Okay, go!" I responded, unnecessarily I might add, because she had already left along with her two pals.

Just as I was starting to point out the day's lesson which I had written on the chalkboard, these same girls rushed back in, and continued the rant at the top of their lungs. I asked them to settle down a couple of times. They wouldn't, and continued to make loud protests within three feet of my face. I then told them to report to the Office, and happened to touch one girl's arm as she brushed by me. They rushed out. Five or ten minutes later, two Administrators came to the door, bringing the girls back, asking what had happened. I was forced to try to explain their behavior while the rest of the class listened with interest, as you can imagine. No sooner had I started to speak than one of the girls declared in a loud and sobbing manner that I had pushed her and in the struggle had caught her earring which had torn from her ear. She punctuated her story with the evidence of a bleeding, albeit slightly, of some blood on her ear. My face made a grimace, I am sure, because I was totally unprepared for this and, as far as I could remember, had not come within two feet of her ears. One Administrator said, "BE THAT AS IT MAY, you must stay in the classroom. " I don't recall the rest.

I had been accused, judged, and given my punishment (i.e. having these girls returned to my classroom for the rest of the period) without my saying a word, and the rest of the class was delighted. Why didn't I walk out, you may well ask? I guess I was too stunned. I know we needed the money. It wasn't much different from much of the disrespect I had suffered over the years. I recall the incident here to illustrate how your credibility as a teacher, an adult, and a supposed colleague was treated by an uncaring administration that knows where the weakest link is and is prepared to use it. So much for professionalism, understanding, and respect. It is tantamount to parents fighting in front of their children. Discipline goes out the window. In this case, Education had left several years before!

I have taught thousands of students from widely different backgrounds and have found few that can do successful, thinking work in a noisy room where others are busily walking or running around, shoving and pushing each other while taunting the harassed teacher who is vainly trying to keep order.

Most of the modern rules and guidelines about student and classroom management have come from psychological and social constructs that have long since been discredited. One case in point is from my daughter's third year Psychology class in 1986. A study conducted under scientific conditions found that "Punishment, to be effective for children, must be as severe as possible without being cruel THE VERY FIRST TIME." If you delay the punishment of a misdemeanor by any length of time, or it must be referred to a higher authority, it only teaches the miscreant that bad behavior succeeds and they go on to more and worse things. Ted Byfield, one of Alberta's main commentators on schools and discipline having spent a lifetime involved in schools, wrote that "The more we discourage using violence to discipline children the more violent our society becomes." (*Western Standard*, July 11, 2005) Rudy Guliani, the mayor of New York City in the 1990's tried an entirely new tactic to reduce crime in his city. Instead of going after only the main criminals, he started by severely punishing the young criminals, including vandalism and graffiti artists. "No broken window" became a watchword for New York crime prevention. Low and behold, within a few years crime had been reduced by 40%, and New York became one of the safest big cities in the United States. The certainly didn't accomplish this remarkable achievement by counseling these "behavior problems" while supplying them with multiple societal reasons for their "unacceptable" behavior. Even the rhetoric must be scaled down so as not to affect their self-esteem.

And don't think that the other students are oblivious to the results of such behavior. Boys, especially, quickly catch on to the extra attention these miscreants receive from the powers that be, as well as the sudden notoriety emanating from their school buddies. It begins to seem like hero worship. More and more they begin to emulate these behaviors. Meanwhile any action the teacher tries to take must be approved by the "bosses" and sometimes right in front of the rest of the class. More often, however, the natural curiosity of the child can figure out whose in charge by playing one side against the other.

Many children are masters at this art. Witness the proliferation of programs such as "SuperNanny" and "Dr. Phil". These experts in modification of child behavior try to diagnose why children are out of control in the home and to help the beleaguered parents to deal with their progeny. These are generally very young, pre-school children who display an amazing (and horrifying to me) degree of temper combined with parent abuse. The main lesson to be learned is that parents must present a united front and NEVER disagree about punishments in front of the children.

Girls tend to be more cooperative than boys in the short run, but can be equally or more vicious in the long run. During one of the teacher conventions that I attended, a lawyer for the Teachers' Union warned us in no uncertain terms that the biggest number of Sexual Assault accusations came from Grade 4 girls. My husband, also a teacher, soon learned never to speak to a young lady alone in the room with the door closed. That could easily turn out to be an accusation of sexual assault. And those accusations came to mean you as a teacher were generally considered guilty until proven innocent. Upon accusation, the teachers is immediately removed from the classroom (with pay if you are lucky) and must try to find some way to discredit these charges. Moreover, judges admonish lawyers for the defense not to harass or emotionally upset the accuser. A friend of mine recounted his tragic experience from just such an accusation. He suffered a heart attack as a result. Several teachers have found themselves not only out of a job, but with their certificates removed. A career and sometimes a lifetime passion has come to a dismal close.

Many of the violent actions by students have been covered up in the past. In fact, few of hundreds of incidents have made it into the public eye, or else the incident has been toned down mightily. For example, yesterday, September 9, 2006, shots were fired at students in a Calgary High School. The item appeared in small print on page 4 of Section B while the front page had such startling articles as *Hot Job Market, Harper to push elected Senate*. How does it happen that the age-old impasse on Senate reform has front page exposure while violence in our school get buried on page 4?

Only a few of these incidents over the years have made it into the newspapers and/or newscasts. One of these involved students' who spiked their teacher's water with a chemical. She was taken to the poison centre for treatment, (September 2, 1992). In May, 2002, a deliberate killing in a Calgary schoolyard by a Young Offender (1992) was classified as an "isolated incident" as was a murder by classmates of a young man at a Halloween party, 1996. A young man had his little finger partially cut off from a fight between rival school gangs. In 2005, some Calgary high school students received threats through the Internet similar to what happened at Columbine High School in Colorado. *Cyberbullying Widespread, students say,* screams a headline in the Calgary Herald , April 16, 2005. That item appeared in a more prominent place, I surmise because it concerned an **American** black mark, which our mass media seems to delight in exposing.

Despite the efforts to low-key any reports of school violence, more of them seem to be occurring more often. In May of 2007 another report of a school shooting resulting in death occurred in Toronto. A teacher has set up a website trying to find an answer to schoolyard and related bullying. (www.bullying.org) Are parents becoming more worried? I know I would be if it was my child, or grandchildren for that matter.

One of the many incidents that didn't make it into the glare of the public eye happened in a high school familiar to my experience. Seventeen arrests were made in a few weeks when drugs, drug paraphernalia, and illegal weapons were found in lockers. However, the charges were basically dismissed because the authorities who attempted to make the arrests had not asked for permission from the student in order to open his locker. In that same school, two teachers found themselves in the middle of fight between rival drug gangs, getting somewhat beat up in the melee. No action was taken and the event was covered up. One teacher went on long term stress leave and eventually left town. A recent documentary in 2007 visited the subject of attacks on teachers and other school personnel. Rumours abound, but it is extremely difficult to get any details.

When I ran for School Trustee in 1992, I talked to several people who tearfully recounted suicides of their teenage children which they believed were due to bullying by schoolmates. In March, 2000, a student jumped off the Patullo Bridge in B.C. after leaving a long note saying he was doing this because his classmates tormented him unmercifully. A few months later, a young girl hanged herself in her bedroom stating a similar reason. (*Readers" Digest*, October, 2001). The school's normal answer to these behaviors, apart from claiming they are "isolated incidents" and covering them up, are to punish both the bully and the one who fights back in the same manner. What a sentence for the victim! No wonder some of them take the only way out they can contemplate. Good-bye, cruel world.

Bullying has been identified as a major problem in many if not most schools throughout both Canada and United States. I guess bullying has always been part and parcel of childhood institutions, but there is no denying it is becoming more and more serious as the years go by. I maintain the whole Top-Down style of Administration is mostly to blame. I know that any actions I took to try to interfere caused me a great deal of grief and censure from my bosses. They did not seem to want to know about the problem because, possibly, it made their school look bad. I don't know how many times I almost choked while an Administrator queried me rhetorically, "The kids in this school are really, really nice kids, aren't they?" Lying is not one of my favorite pastimes.

It is interesting to note that as I write this on September 12, 2006, the Rutherford show is airing a show dealing with bullying in the classroom and the school. Heather Forsyth, the guest, stated that she just returned from an international conference on school bullying. Their major recommendation was that bullying should be classified and treated as a criminal offence, not as a behavioral aberration which can be corrected through behavior modification. This same sentiment is echoed in an article in *Reader's Digest*, October, 2001. "In considering a school for your child, you should ask the principal if it has an anti-bullying policy and, if it does, how well it works. If you are told, 'We don't have that problem here.' Don't believe it. The problem exists in all schools." I concur. The problem exists, and it is incumbent on the adults to take action. In other words, bullying behavior should be punished, not talked out or "understood" in terms of life circumstances. Bravo! Maybe now, something positive will be done. Furthermore, the victim should NEVER be treated the same as the perpetrator. Am I holding my breath? Not yet.

A few examples remain of principals who have done the right thing and cleaned up his/her school. I give them full credit. However, it serves no positive purpose for principals or others higher in the bureaucracy to contradict and countermand the actions of a teacher in the classroom, unless there is actual physical abuse by the teacher witnessed by another adult or several students in separate testimony. Be careful, children as a small group ARE capable of conspiring against a teacher or other adult. I have been a target of just such a situation as have others. One situation I was witness to ended up in a courtroom challenge. This teacher won her case after hiring her own personal lawyer to question the three opposing witnesses who **SWORE UNDER OATH** that **SHE** had been the one who had been the abuser. Most of us cannot afford to take our grievances this far.

A personal discussion between teacher and administrator as colleagues as to how to handle a situation would be in order, I believe. However, an overt reversal of a teacher's decision only serves to belittle the teacher in her/his students' eyes. It is never a good idea to air your differences about consequences for misbehavior in front of children as most parents have painfully learned when dealing with their our own children. Why then should it be good for school children to learn that the classroom teacher's word is never the last one?

It took me many failures to realize that the administration was not there to support my efforts at taming the disruptive actions of the class clown or the defiant words of a class leader. "Don't take any wrong-headed behavior from anyone in the class. Send him/her to the Office and we'll deal with it," were the words of the principal or assistant principal. Naively at first, I believed him or her. WRONG ANSWER, I soon learned to my grief. Without fail, any student I sent to the Office would be result in a humiliating event. Just as the rest of the class was settling down, back in would march the miscreant or miscreants smirking and triumphant, without so much as a knock on the door. Before I could venture a question, the rejoinder would come, "The principal/assistant principal sent me back." With that statement my position as teacher in charge of classroom management was destroyed. I was, obviously, just a minion, a servant with little status, definitely having less authority not only than the principal, but also of the students as well, since they had the right to enter (and exit I might add) my classroom at any time they chose. To add injury to insult, I would then be required to spend after school hours writing out my explanation as to what happened. Never, over my forty-six year span of teaching did I ever have anyone follow up to these disciplinary efforts in a positive way.

Soon I resorted to the method used by many other teachers. Handle it yourself. The corridors became a good indicator of how tight the discipline was in any school. By that I mean that one could judge how effectively the teachers had managed to "motivate" their students by how many were sitting in the corridors particularly in the later afternoon. Few teachers took the opportunity to refer the student to the Administration, preferring instead to let them cool their heels in the corridor until they could get a minute to deal with it themselves. I recall one rather humorous occasion when a water fight ensued between warring classmates while we teachers were busily occupied. I realize parents may be incredulous and doubtful about these statements, but I see no reason to continue hiding the truth and pretending discipline is well under control.

Several different methods were used by career teachers to deal with this ineffective Top-Down approach yet still continue to hold onto their jobs. How did they manage? First of all, you identify what is the most important thing. The answer was obvious ... keep the students in school; whether they learn anything or not is of secondary importance. Some teachers became masters at music, magic, joke-telling, or finding entertaining ways to conduct lessons; a high energy strategy at the best of times. Bribery, for example candy rewards, was another method. Others, generally in high school, spent much of September identifying several of the ringleaders who showed obvious signs of defying authority and disinterest in learning, to coin a phrase. Incidents were documented carefully. When the requisite number of occasions was recorded off (as high as 14 or 15 items, I kid you not) he or she would go to the Counselors clutching the written documentation, insisting that said student be removed from "my" classroom. The documentation proved that the Administration had little choice but to have these targeted students transferred to another classroom or another school due to "personality conflicts".

Ah, the sweet flavor of peace and tranquility in the pursuit of learning for the rest of the semester. Ah, not quite. Teaching is a demanding job. Well, do I remember the two or three hours a weeknight my husband or I spent marking papers. Today's students do not self-mark for those of you old enough to remember expectations from "the good old days". Everything must be marked by the teacher, except maybe for quick quizzes as a class opener. Later, there appeared the Multiple Choice Scanning Machines, a godsend for correcting multiple choice or other yes-no answers, but definitely limited when it came to higher level learning.

The most rewarding strategy was for you as a teacher to aim for fewer and fewer students, better yet, no students at all. Get out of the classroom and get a position as Administrator yourself, or the best yet, Counselor. To add injury to insult, if you succeeded you usually were paid more. No wonder few really good teachers stayed the course inside the classroom.

Getting back to the limitations of Top-Down administration, how can learning be advanced by having people not in the classroom make decisions about how you should treat your young charges? In fact many of these experts have NEVER been in a classroom for any length of time. I know, I know, there must be a boss, so say all the management models. Here comes the big BUT … If the teacher has a boss, shouldn't it be the parents, not someone in the hierarchy who is protected from all consequences of wrong-headed decisions by distance, bureaucracy, secretaries, lawyers, and full funding?

The major consequence for the teacher might be that she/he lacks one less student, maybe at a requisite loss of the dollar amount for that one student. This would constitute a better balance in my opinion than the present model which consists of paying the same salary to all teachers regardless of how many students they teach. In fact, many of the most highly paid "teachers" teach no students at all. Many if not most career teachers at present, specifically aim for this nirvana .... yes, dear reader, a teacher salary and benefits without the bother of filtering it through a group of unruly students. Consequently, we have evolved into the impossible situation where you have bosses who have little or no idea how difficult it is trying to teach while the classroom is in chaos. The usual price paid is that education suffers, as witness by our abominable rates of real literacy and knowledge by our graduates.

This argument is usually counteracted by pointing out how many scholarships and academic awards have been attained by our students. That argument begs the question. Public education must take the responsibility for the totality of education among all the graduates. And *that* record is appalling. Instead of two percent illiteracy in our population (which equates to the percentage of the population with very low intelligence quotients) studies show 25% are close to illiterate, yet have spent ten or more years of sitting in a our classrooms. More about Accountability will be dealt with in Chapter V.

The issue of corporal punishment has been bandied about ever since the late 1960's. Few would dispute that caning as per Charles Dickens is acceptable. In fact, you would be hard-pressed to find anyone who thinks this is actually a civilized way of treating anyone under your protection. That being said, abolition of any kind of physical punishment became the goal of zealots, many of whom did not have children of their own or were not on the front line in a classroom. Mary Van Stalk wrote a book called *The Battered Child* in 1972 advocating abolition of spanking saying it only resulted in children becoming more aggressive. How she would explain the present exhibitions of aggressive behavior by a couple of generations of unspanked toddlers becomes an intriguing question. She also stated that, far from the family being the most caring environment, more people die in the family than in any other way. Wow! I put this article in my Horrors File. This kind of emotional evidence untainted by real research has been the impetus behind our lemming-like march to ban corporal punishment.

By the mid 1970's, corporal punishment had been disallowed with legal repercussions for teachers all over the western provinces, except perhaps for some isolated communities often within strong Christian strongholds. From then on classroom discipline seemed to deteriorate rapidly. I would hardly say that the abolition of strapping can be pinpointed as the only reason, perhaps not even the main reason, but I contend that this act bears some of the blame. I have been told repeatedly, from adult men particularly, that a strapping in public school was the best lesson they ever got in learning good behavior. From my viewpoint this whole issue should be revisited based on true scientific investigation

In the early 1990,s, I choose the topic of Corporal Punishment as a research project for a graduate class. Study after study proved inconclusive or somewhat indicative of the positive effects of corporal punishment when handled carefully. However, not content with contributing to teachers' headaches, the zealots continued in their obsession until Child Protection from Abuse Laws were implemented across Canada legally threatening parents who chose to use these methods *with their own children*. These zealots were undismayed or unable to connect the fact that the majority of the Young Offenders had come through the Social Services sector of society. That is to say, if these so-called "experts" know so much about raising children, how does it happen that they are so unsuccessful at raising decent citizens from children entirely under their control? Moreover, the issue of amounts of money available for this job is hardly as big an issue for social services as it is for the average family. If dollars are the main answer (as its adherents aver) the Social Services departments should be far more effective at raising decent and contributing citizens since they have much more money to spend per child than parents in a private home. It never ceases to amaze me that the governments seem to operate on the principle that the more you fail the more you should continue blindly down the same path, throwing more and more money at the problem. Has anyone in the bureaucracy ever heard of the adage " Think outside the box"?

Applying corporal punishment needs to be done very carefully and sensitively in order to have the desired effect of changing a person's behavior. It should not be the measure of first or random choice, but only for serious disrespect and/or assault on others. For very young children, it is the most effective method for changing dangerous behavior in my experience. Without thinking, I gave my kids a swat on the backside when they did something really foolish like running into the street, biting a playmate, or striking someone with a hard object. I saw other respectable people doing it as well. Usually this affair ended up with a weeping child running to jump on a parent lap, begging to be hugged. The lesson was quickly learned for the moment, leaving such a deep impression that it was generally not repeated. As far as it scarring a person's psyche, I have not seen the evidence. I understand that Stalin, Hitler, and Saddam Hussein had very abusive childhood experiences, but a swat on the bum is a far cry from what they experienced. I know we can find the proper evidence for effective discipline, but we must stop trusting the self-appointed experts and look for the objective facts.

Did the top educrats care about looking seriously at the results of little or no consequences after years of this soft-handed, top-down approach? Not to my knowledge. Laws, regulations and punishments were handed down from on high. Teachers were forbidden to take matters into their own hands when it came to deciding on any punishment except for talking to and counseling their charges.

Rudolf Dreikur, a child psychologist, and other people anxious to understand what *really* works, advised, in essence "When it comes to punishment, the worst thing you as the authority can do is to use a lot of words. Save communication for positive interaction between student and teacher or parent and child. Take action. Say as little as possible.

Children need to see a big difference in your behavior between their right and wrong actions." (A New Approach to Discipline: *Logical Consequences,* Rudolf Dreikur, c1950)

In a few tragic examples, teachers lost their jobs and sometimes their accreditation, parents were reported to the social services and had to explain their actions. The. Luyendyks' story became front page news in the early1980's. This couple had spent much of their lives caring for unwanted children most of whom turned out to be model citizens very grateful to their foster parents. One young lady decided to take advantage of the new laws against child abuse to accuse them of physical abuse because of their use of corporal punishment. The Social Services spent thousands of dollars prosecuting this case, and the judge concurred. Their Valley Farm Home was shut down and Mr. Luyendyk spent some time in jail. Several years later the young lady recanted her accusations and tried to undo the damage, but this became low value news. Regardless, the damage could not be undone to these people; and the Zealots, notwithstanding, continued to pursue the original goals.

Since then there have been several horror stories due to bureaucratic bungling or single-minded pursuit of an "idealistic' objective, that seems to extend, like the horizon "forever and forever as I move". The Matherthorpe fiasco involving a falsely-accused Day Care Center near Saskatoon, Saskatchewan comes to mind, as does the Alymer (Ontario) case where seven children were ripped out of the arms of their parents because the parents believed in corporal punishment.

Canadians like to think of themselves as sane, compassionate, civilized people who never go to extremes on any issue, especially actions. These actions, on the parts of anti-spanking Zealots, belies and buries this self-description, or should I say self-denial? Whatever happened to individual rights as regards our own children, a part of life that immediately impacts on schools and teachers. Should majority vote decide everything? After all, the majority of the Germans elected Hitler, and it seems our mindset seems to be that anything goes as long as the majority of people have okayed it. Canada was supposed to be founded on individual rights which superceded majority rule. Majorities can be as hurtful as any dictatorships as history has proved. Think about it.

It is easy to criticize, but how should we correct this? You may well ask. Here is my answer. Teachers should be masters of their own classrooms, as should parents in their own homes. The only time the law should interfere is when there is physical abuse (including sexual abuse). To balance this authority, no child should be forced to go to a specific school or attend a specific classroom, as long as the parents support their child. Voucher education would solve the logistics of this approach. Concurrently, teachers must accept their students in the beginning, but do not have to keep them in the classroom if, for a stated, written reason, that teacher wishes to have them removed. Naturally, this action must be explained openly to the parents, possibly with the attendance of the student in question, but not necessarily the Principal. In the classroom, the teacher is his/her own boss. In other words, an Administrator cannot override a teacher's decision regarding disciplining a student. Administrators would be there to administrate, that is, concentrate on the overall smoothness of operation, make rules for and monitor behavior in corridors and common areas, and take care of the minutia of day to day operations. Mostly they must try to make things as easy and pleasant as possible for the students and teachers. Let's give control and choice on all sides, a policy which has stood the test of time and experience in providing the most agreeable situation. My prediction ... it will also cost the least amount of dollars as well, and produce the best educated populous.

CHAPTER THREE – MANDATORY UNIONS

"I sit on a man's back, choking him and making him carry me, and yet assure myself and him that I am very sorry for him and wish to lighten his load by all possible means – except by getting off his back."

Count Lev Tolstoi, 1828-1910

When I first started teaching in 1959 I was very intrigued by the fact that I did not have to worry about my teaching salary. Participation in the Teachers' Union was mandatory for all public school teachers. This included principals and other school administrators whether teaching or not. During my adolescence I earned a few dollars here and there by babysitting and helping with the school caretaking. I knew how difficult it was to ask for an increase from individuals whom I knew did not welcome the request; therefore I welcomed this arrangement of a union handling the delicate matter of salary and matters relating to earnings. How nice that someone else would do it for me.

The spokesperson at our Teachers' College explained how collective bargaining worked and proudly displayed a chart showing the increases that had recently been negotiated. However, I did wonder who was paying for this largess. Yes, I realized it was through taxes, but didn't everyone complain about the taxes they had to pay? And wasn't I going to have to pay them as well?

Little did I realize how fundamental these questions were, and how they would impact the whole government role in the future. For decades now, organizations, companies, and individuals expect to budget inflation into their calculations for the coming year. Projections become astronomical when you extrapolate those figures for twenty or thirty years into the future. This cannot continue indefinitely, but do unions, particularly public service unions, seem to care? They tend to avoid the question at all costs.

Hundreds of private companies, small and large, over the last forty years have gone bankrupt because of union wage and benefit demands. The Chrysler Corporation in 1980 faced just this prospect. Lee Iaccoca, who became the new CEO at this time, disclosed in his book that there were more Chrysler workers on retirement, sick leave, or vacation than were actually working on the assembly line. Fortunately, he managed to forestall the bankruptcy (challenging the company by taking a salary himself of only one dollar for the first year), but many smaller companies have been forced to sell out their stock at huge discounts, and hand pink slips to all their employees. In Calgary, the Burns Company and Molson Brewery were two well-known companies that folded because of union demands. Pollsters tell us that two out of three enterprises fail in the first three years, often because of employee demands. In recent years, the high cost of extra benefits has been cited as one of the main contributing factors to companies going under. There is a whole industry now in Liquidation sales and takeovers.

Mandatory unionism has been very troublesome for the private sector, but its effects pale by comparison when translated into the public arena of service. It was strange that our leaders did not foresee this happening. As public service unionism became the established norm, governments felt the need to expand their powers of control. Admittedly, this is not the only reason for expansion of government control, but it was a significant factor. Over the fifty plus years of my experience it has become normal for governments to control through taxation 45 percent of our total earning power, with no end in sight. (Report issued by AM770 Radio on April 30, 2007 and the Fraser Institute) Back in the 1960's the percentage of government demand on one's earning power was approximately one-half of that at 25 percent. When you take into consideration that government revenues have increased from approximately nine billion in 1965 to 222.2 billion dollars in 2007, an increase of 1500 percent, it boggles the mind. In comparable statistics, it used to cost us $450 per person per year to fund the Federal government, now it costs us $6720. (data from National Citizens' Coalition)

In our present time, public service unions have the ability not only to bankrupt a company, but in actuality to hold the whole citizenry to ransom. And at times they have done so. It happened in New Zealand in the late 1970's, it is happening in France, and most of the other former "free" countries of Europe. It is a strange thing about human nature ... we have great reluctance to give up something of value in our lives for which we think someone else will be paying.

Another question arises, ... has our quality of life due to government largesse increased in the same proportion? I think not, by a long shot. We now have government interfering all aspects of our lives up to and including how we treat our children. For example, when I started teaching, albeit with only one year of teacher training where now the average is four years, my salary was approximately the same as that of a telephone operator, a clerk in a store, a waitress in a restaurant, or a secretary. There was an egalitarianism about relations among workers from differing vocations. If I were teaching now, employers in the private sector would be hard pressed to pay me one quarter of what I could make as a teacher. As a result, there is measure of shame in doing these kinds of work. Consequently, we have evolved a permanent underclass in these private service jobs, exactly the opposite of what these draconian measures of forced unionism were supposed to accomplish. My colleagues might argue that teaching is a much more difficult and valuable job, but I tend to disagree having worked in both sectors. It seems the amount of money one earns results in the value of your job. That could be the criterion under capitalism, but definitely not under statism. I'll leave that argument for another time.

The bosses of big unions have the ability to withhold vulnerable services from huge sectors of the population. Moreover, these services are, in themselves, government monopolies. The regular population cannot even purchase these outside the system without going outside the law. Up to the present most of these public service strikes have given rise to huge protests by the general populace, demanding that government settle the strike immediately. I cannot stifle the feeling that protests play directly into the hands of the union bosses. Education is among these services as we are all aware. Our children are held to ransom.

Governments at all levels have implemented "innovative" ideas and policies to counteract the effects of these strikes except for the logical policy of making union membership strictly a voluntary choice. We now know of such mind-boggling ideas as "illegal strikes", "mandatory services without ability to strike legally", and "mediators" to settle strikes when the two parties cannot agree within certain time limits. In my experience, dear reader, there has not been one of these illegal strikes or "work to rule's" that has sided with the beleaguered taxpayer. The big man is still on our backs, and unwilling to let go. Unions were supposed to improve the lot for all workers. The opposite has happened in terms of mandatory public service unions, not only in Canada, but in country after country that has implemented these policies. The power has merely shifted to union bosses as the final arbiters, who have proved as heartless as any captain of industry or sweatshop boss. As it applies to teaching, I know that the taxpayer have been forgotten in the rush to get larger and larger salaries, benefits and days off for its members. As a substitute teacher, I stood last in line, but nevertheless made better money than I could have in most other temporary jobs. Among my peers I was treated as a second class citizen. I believe this bad attitude was based on the fact that a substitute makes about one-half what a regular teacher makes, and enjoys few of the extra benefits provided in the union contract. An article appearing in *Maclean's* magazine, April 2, 2007, exposes this same phenomenon for university contract workers.

I can attest to the truth of the *Maclean's* article from my experience during the ugly days after the National Energy Program which nearly broke Alberta's economy. Thousands of people were thrown out of work, or cut back to the extent where paying the monthly bills became a major problem. I was on the Sub List and taking every job I could get, on a minutes notice. The Calgary Board of Education was inundated with applications by downsized professionals wanting to get on this same list. The Substitute Teacher List expanded to 1800 persons because it had been their policy to put add names as certified teachers requested. Being on the Sub List was not a highly desired goal, to put it mildly. Soon none of us were getting called to work because of this glut of possible temporary employees. By putting much pressure on our union leaders, we managed to persuade the Board to limit the List to 600 persons, which made things somewhat easier.

Now how does this relate to university contract teachers? In my travels from school to school I began to meet sub teachers with engineering degrees, doctorates, masters' degrees and other top qualifications. One day I met a man who informed me in casual conversation that this was his job on Mondays, Wednesdays, and Fridays; the other two days he taught at the University of Calgary on contract. He was seriously thinking of giving up his contract job to be available on the other two days per week. Why? Because the pay as a substitute teacher was better than his contract teaching! More satisfying? No, but when you are trying to raise two sons the money becomes a higher priority than dignity or societal respect. The article in *Maclean's* seemed to blame "too little government funding", as most of the major media tend to do. I believe the greater reason for this topsy turvy situation rests with Closed Shop unionism which has raised and continues to raise the pay and benefits for its members thus completely subverting the value of what a worker actually does on the job.

There are people who have recognized the limitations of making employment too expensive. Jennifer Roback Morse, a research writer for the Hoover Institute wrote in 2004 that "... some of our illegal immigration problems arise from government regulations mandating unsustainable wages and benefits." Many Canadians will write this off by saying it is strictly an American problem. Hardly true. Later in the article, she states, "All over Europe, immigrants form North Africa and the Midddle East do these jobs. These Muslim immigrants, barred from the higher-class jobs, are angry about their exclusion." ("Where Jobs are illegal, only illegals will have jobs by J. R. Morse in *Calgary Herald*, March 4, 2004) That anger spilled over in 2005 into riots in many parts of France, one of the countries that is immensely proud, whether justly or not, of its strong social policies and charitable attitudes.

Even mandating minimum wages can have a deleterious effect on entry level job-seekers, or those wishing a less than fulltime, less demanding employment. For example, those homemakers or pensioners who would like to contribute to children's education, are excluded from doing such jobs in the schools as lunchroom or schoolyard supervision, because of union demands. Many of us would like to help out in these capacities or perhaps become teacher assistants on a volunteer basis, but are prevented from doing so because of union considerations. It appears the Union is suspicious of anyone who may take away from its mandate, or provide a comparison with possible contributions from individuals outside its direct control. I believe education would benefit greatly by adopting a more global view, rather than insisting on mandating the roles and wages of peripheral workers. These mandates have increased the cost, and very possibly, the effectiveness of public education.

Another article, which seems relevant here, appeared in the *Las Vegas Review*, March 4, 2004. Rod Paige of the *Washington Post* speculated that "The union-dominated status quo is impervious to change." This was not a startling fact to me. Having started teaching in 1959 in Grade One using the frustrating and non-successful Dick-Jane look-say method of teaching reading I encountered great reluctance from the powers that be to acknowledge this failure. Even when this method was discredited, there was no return to the original phonics method which had worked for thousands of citizens in the early days of Western Canada. Modifications have occurred over time, but the method remains basically phonics. Somehow it seems impossible for a government, influenced greatly by a strong union to admit its failure and return, at least temporarily to something that has worked well in the past, or to implement an entirely new and proven approach.

Meanwhile, mandatory unionism seems to have constricted what subjects a school or teacher can offer to students. On a visit to Ukraine in 2001, I toured a 19th century village heritage site. Much to my surprise (having swallowed the dictum that Ukraine had never been one of the "advanced" nations of the world) one of the buildings I visited was two room school house and teacher's cottage. The teacher's job consisted, not only of the basic subjects of reading, writing, mathematics, history, geography, but also of music instruction (in at least one instrument such as violin or tsimbali), and art and art appreciation. Moreover, being provided with a cottage and place for a garden, the schoolmaster was expected to instruct his students in the homemaking arts of gardening and housekeeping. Naturally, all caretaking work was also the sphere of the schoolmaster and his students. I'm talking here about a small, remote village in western Ukraine in the mid 1800's. Needless to say, I felt very inadequate as to my duties as a teacher. That is not to say that teachers should be expected to competently teach all those subjects but it does point out that years ago with far less resources, parents and teachers were able to provide good education without any government funds. It is ludicrous to believe that without tax largesse our children would be illiterate savages.

Government Teachers' Unions seem to feel it is their mandate to cut down on the responsibilities normally done by their membership. Recently, I have been nonplussed to discover that lunchtime supervision is not the responsibility of the school in some jurisdictions, but must be paid for out of the parents' purse. This new non-responsibility of the teaching staff applies for all the five to eleven year olds who are forced to go to school by law. Most parents are working at jobs outside the home so are not available to supervise their children at this time. Besides which, noon break hardly affords enough time for a child to make it home and back before classes start again in the afternoon. Some schools took it upon themselves to recruit parents, grandparents, et cetera to volunteer for this chore, or hired part-time, people to fill in on an hour by hour basis. The Union stepped in, declaring that these positions must be unionized in order to afford proper insurance protection. Naturally, the cost escalated. A few parents made a fuss, and refused to pay. In some cases School Boards have sent bill collectors to harass them. So far no children have been turned out into the streets for non-payment of this fee I am told, but children have been embarrassed and humiliated, some even in front of their peers. I consider this treatment arrogant and non professional, brought about primarily because of the ironclad laws surrounding mandatory unionism. It is comforting to be informed about a new organization, Parents for Public Education, which is preparing to take the School Board to court saying this ruling of pay for lunchtime supervision is against the School Act of Alberta. I know from experience that lunchroom supervision has been so integral a part of the school's responsibility that it made me incredulous until I saw the actual newsletter from my granddaughter's school.

Workers in the public service now are envied by most of the population. These are the "good" jobs because of their high salaries and, more importantly their excellent benefits. Governments are hard-pressed to stop the demands for more. Have the public service unions backed off, and lessened their demands? Exactly the opposite. Every year or two new contracts are negotiated for months, services are withdrawn often at crucial times, and advertisements cry out about the greater " needs" of these groups. By and large, the major media in newspapers, magazines, and television support the myths that these public service groups are poorly compensated for the work they do. I cite as a current example a letter to the editor by a teacher (*Calgary Herald,* September 8, 2007) chosen as the special "Letter of the Day" complaining bitterly about the unfair complaints people *may* be making on their (the teachers) recent demands for double digit increases. "… why not turn your sights on the many six-figure executive salaries and bonuses .., she asks " Imagine that! Teachers' salaries should be comparable to those of CEO's. If she was teaching in the private sector, I could have no quarrel, but a teacher in the public system … how arrogant can you get? The leader of a teachers' union recently commented to a reporter that unions have a right to large inputs into the education system because "..we're the experts…" Eventually this arrogance and intransigence will break the taxpayer and the economy.

Closed Shop Union participation, (which became law in Alberta in 1936) is anathema to long term success for any employer. Unions have done good things in the beginning when they were not mandatory. Since then they have become large pressure and lobby groups. The National Teachers' Union in the United States is said to be the biggest financial supporter of the Democratic Party. The Ontario Teachers' Pension Fund is one of the largest pools of money in that province with the corresponding power such money affords. The upper echelons of this organization overwhelming support the New Democratic Party or the "progressive" Liberal candidates. Other closed shop unions have done likewise. This means that you as a union member had no choice in how your compulsory dues were used, a big chink in the fundamental principal of private property rights and laws. Even though several individuals and groups (notably, the National Citizens' Coalition) has gone as far as the Supreme Court to invalidate this practice, it still remains in place. Most union members ignore or blithely accept this intrusion into their basic freedoms and rights. It appears that might is always right. Majority rule trumps individual rights and freedoms. In other words, the majority can always dip into your minority pockets with impunity.

In regard to how these intrusive laws have affected education, this has meant that costs have spiraled upward to become triple what most jobs pay in the private sector. Teachers' unions juggle the books to denounce these details. They falsely compare teachers and administrators pay with those of CE0's of large companies or with policemen or firemen. Countering arguments are ignored. After all, CEO's do not get the holidays or the hours that teachers take for granted. They can and are fired or replaced when the company does not perform well enough to keep shareholders happy. Policemen and firemen put their lives on the line, a call far above what is expected of most teachers. Besides, they also belong to mandatory civil service unions and have flexed their muscle from time to time, sometimes without merit.

It is hard to counter the argument that being a teacher is the best job for a parent when you consider the positive dovetailing of hours and holidays that teachers have over parents employed in any other profession. Add to this mix the tenure that most teachers enjoy after two years of employment with one School Board, and you truly have a prized position. We will deal with the question of accountability, or lack of it, in another chapter

The Teachers' Pensions is another case in point. On August 24, 2004, a review of pensions for Alberta public teachers was reported on the Dave Rutherford show. In 1939, soon after the Alberta Teachers' Association (ATA) became mandatory, the Government of Alberta agreed to provide three percent to the accumulated Pension Plan. In 1948, the figure was raised to four percent. In 1956, a huge jump brought the public's share to matching the teachers' contributions by an equal amount, and to guarantee its continuation should there be a shortfall. Later, in 1966 and 1987 further increases were demanded by the ATA lobby and granted by an embattled government. Then in 1992 (at which time I was a participant in this settlement) the "unfunded liability was further enhanced by the Alberta Government. Need I remind you, dear reader, that this step was taken just before Premier Ralph Klein introduced his plan to eliminate the Alberta debt of twenty eight billion dollars. Admittedly, the teachers still in the system had to kick in additional moneys as well, but the Alberta debt had become a central issue for the citizens. Was it an issue for the Union? No mention was made of it at the meeting

A few economists (those dreary number crunchers) warned that "benefits" were fast becoming the biggest stumbling blocks to businesses and government services. This fact did not seem to faze the public service. If you examine the historical record you will note that the monetary demands and settlements of government servants became ever more strident and incessant, with the concomitant disregard for the difficulty of the average wage earner or business to compete. Meanwhile, various teachers' unions began flexing their muscles in other areas. Imagine, having that kind of a hold on the public purse, without the balancing effect of having to pay for it. Every king, emperor, or czar of the Past would be envious. Even these old-style dictators felt the need be nice to the various earls, landlords, and vassals in order to get the necessary money and public support. Not the Education system. Schools became completely controlled from the Top Down. There was little need for the people at the top to answer to their customers, the parents as the guardians of their children. The same applied to the teachers in the schools. If you wanted to advance in your section, you had to please the principal, the superintendent, or the union hierarchy, forget the parents or the students. Brown-nosing, (officially called mentoring) took on a whole new meaning.

In all this mix we have forgotten the School Boards. They were set up to be the arbiter between the teachers and the parents and the watchdogs for the taxpayers' dollars. How times have changed! Maybe School Boards were watchdogs in the past, but for at least the last quarter century they have forgotten their major role and become another front for various pressure groups such as the teachers' unions, the supporting staff unions, the caretakers' unions, and the demands of parent groups for more schools, more bussing, more, more, more. The wailing for more and more and more funding is deafening. It almost seems badmouthing our Premier must be a prerequisite for becoming a school board member. Maybe it is because many of the members of the School Boards are retired teachers or their spouses or "boy/girl friends". One recent Board chairperson was the past president of the local teachers' union. How biased is that.

A horror story from the other side of Canada has illustrated how powerful unions can overrule all our sacred cows even Safety. The Montreal Larger School Board was forced to re-instate a teacher who had been convicted of murdering his wife by beating her to death. He was supported in his suit for re-instatement by his Teachers' Union who argued that this event had occurred six years earlier and, therefore, was irrelevant. The Human Rights Commission in Quebec ruled in his and the Union's favor despite the fact that he had lied on his application to the Board when asked if he had ever been convicted of a crime. These bodies were able to convince a Commissioner that " ..the teacher.... Has a right to a job". (August 21, 2007, on Rutherford Talk Radio AM770)

In 2006, a public school board member was dismissed from his elected office for having the temerity to suggest his Board was not open to outside examination of its books or debate on its policies. The other members of the Board took him to Court. To bring poison to misery, the Court found in favor of the majority of the Board. Later, the Courts decided he was also not eligible to become a contender for a re-run at this same position. All the media reports I read appeared to agree with the judges in their coverage. Who, then, I ask, is looking out for number one, that is, the much ignored public taxpayer, not even to mention the forgotten student consumer of their products? I think these actions were abominable.

Teachers' contracts have become so complicated it requires professional accountants and mediators to deal with them. The collective agreements are booklet size, at least 50 pages in length and as fascinating to peruse as last night's dishwater. Most people have little knowledge of what's in them, most employees affected read only the parts that pertain to their salaries and benefits. Lawyers and accountants concentrate on details as they come up. The only ones who really know what is in them are the union bosses who have compiled them over the years.

Finally, most discussions regarding contract details are carried on in a highly intimidating manner. The teaching profession in Alberta and Saskatchewan for sure includes principals and administrators in the same bargaining contract as the regular classroom teachers. As a matter of fact the local superintendent is a member of the Teachers' Local as well. These are the people that have a big say in whether you are hired or not, whether you become tenured or not, and whether you get a good teaching load or a really difficult one. Moreover, most of the votes are by a show of hands, even over highly sensitive issues like how much money should be donated to a certain political campaign. I do NOT call this fair or democratic. It is Big Brother using Group pressure and intimidation to put across a point of view.

These conditions relate to employees of many post secondary institutions as well, although I am not familiar with many of the details since I have never been an employee of one for any length of time. Most professors and instructors in these Institutions also belong to unions, and enjoy the comfort and safety of Tenure. Consequently, we have some of the nuttiest ideas being fed to our young adults who must please their instructors in order to get a passing grade. I have personally experienced the angst of sitting through whole courses where my values were battered beyond belief. Confidences shared from young people I know further confirm how insulted and terrified they were as well. What recourse do you have? Very little, especially if the course is mandatory. Discretion usually replaces outrage when you realize that the professor or instructor whom you are questioning is the very same person who decides on your final and largely uncontestable mark. In high school you may have had the right to appeal; in post-secondary you usually don't have even that slim chance to object or question your tester.

Unions are now using intimidating tactics to force unionism on employees even when these people do not request them. Their representatives are allowed to go into a private business and freely talk to employers, hand out literature, and pressure them to sign a document requesting union certification. Walmart continues to be a favorite target of these over-zealous unionists. If employees still prove reluctant, they then continue by harassing them at home. If you think I am exaggerating, examine the case going on in Lively, Ontario, involving seven women employees of the TD Canada Trust bank. They were unionized without their consent on March 29, 2005. In fact, they specifically refused the offers of union "benefits" and had applied to the Canada Industrial Relations Board (CIRB) for Intervener status after union representatives kept harassing them, even making uninvited visits to their homes. The Application to the CRIB had not answered their appeal, except to say it had received it. In desperation they have now requested and are receiving support from the National Citizens' Coalition (NCC).

The NCC is a private, non-profit, non-taxfunded organization which took on Mark Levigne's case against union abuses in the past. He was upset about his Teachers' Union giving money to a political party not of his choosing and without his consent. With their deep pockets the Union kept up this fight for years, going as far as the Supreme Court where they finally won. In the fallout, they came within a whisper of bankrupting the National Citizens' Coalition. This goes to prove that unless you as a citizen have protection from compulsory unionism, you will become a puppet for them, manipulated and coerced for THEIR ends, not yours. People who still believe that forced unionism does nothing but good for workers, must re-examine the facts given the record of the last seventy or so years. Its history is little better than that of many of the dictators and absolute kingships of the past.

This is not what Canada was supposed to be about. Mandatory public service unions should be abolished. In fact, all compulsory unions should be stopped. That is the only fair and democratic way to do things. It is only a question of time before they break the system, and Time has been on the side of this Big Brother throughout my life.

I don't like it.

CHAPTER FOUR – SCHOOL TIME (& MONEY) WASTERS

"The bird of time has but a little way
To flutter – and the bird is on the wing."

Omar Khayyam, *Rubaiyat,* **11th Century**

There are multiple ways to waste time in schools, some over which the teacher has no control. These administrative interruptions include such things as fire drills, lock-down drills, intercom messages, and special school announcements. If these interruptions last only a few minutes they must be marked down is part and parcel of the school day. However, some of them have become so frequent and/ or last so long that they severely interfere with the ongoing learning process.

Number One time-waster, although not necessarily the most egregious one that comes to mind in my school experience, have been the ubiquitous fire drills. Very necessary, I agree, but do they have to occur in the midst of an exam or test? And their frequency in some schools has become a real problem and very costly. Most municipal districts charge several hundred dollars every time the Fire Department is called out on a false alarm. Several times in my experience, nearly adult young people, who are bored with school have made it into a game, especially since now we've evolved a general climate of no real consequences for misbehaving students.. Consequently, these "unscheduled" fire drills have become a considerable cost for the School Board as well as a great way to get out of a test; certainly a great time-waster.

Teachers are expected to check the room, the closets and bathrooms to see that no student is left behind, then follow the students to a designated place for that class's safety area.

Next you must take attendance to see that all the students are accounted for, not an easy task especially for a substitute teacher who is often not even given a class list as well as having been relieved of Roster Duty by a room monitor. While I can see this is a necessary drill, new safety regulations are insisting that this procedure be done more frequently. I wonder exactly how many students in Canada have burned to death in school-related fires in the last fifty years. I know of none. Maybe we should re-examine this drill in terms of frequency and timing. Any student or other person who pulls this off as a prank should face the Logical Consequence of having to pay the cost of the Fire Department call at the very least.

A brand new time waster with much harsher consequences is the "Lock-Down". This new phenomenon has been instituted in many schools because of a school shooting that occurred in Columbine High School in Colorado, spring of 1999 where 12 students and one teacher were shot to death by two students who subsequently committed suicide. A copycat shooting followed later that spring in Taber, Alberta, with the death of Jason Lang. Other similar incidents of note include the one as recently as September 13, 2006, at Dawson College in Montreal (no fatalities), another in Concordia University in Montreal, 1992 (four fatalities). Immediately the above occurrences were linked to the initial tragedy of December, 1989, where 14 women were shot in the Montreal Ecole Poytechnique by a deranged gunman, the son of an Algerian immigrant, Mark Lepine, nee Gamil Gharbi, who openly stated he hated women, possibly because of his troubled family background. Now, all schools suffer because of his heinous act.

It seems there is hardly a month goes by now without a similar tragedy getting front page notice in our modern cities. I refer specifically to school violence and deaths. Previous to 1989 there were only two recorded school fatalities, one in 1978 in Winnipeg (one death, a lover's spat) and Burlington, Ontario, 1975, (one teacher and one student). The situation of school safety seems to have taken a more deadly turn in recent years, especially if you include the horrible events in April, 2007, in West Virginia, where 33 school personnel met their deaths. No records exist of similar tragedies of this type prior to 1989. However, adding it up, altogether, a grand total of 22 people shot to death in Canadian schools since records have been kept, around 1960.

Notwithstanding that these have been terribly tragic events, it does not seem to follow that thousands of students as well as their educational progress should have to suffer to try to avert "even one more death". Educational authorities seem to forget that these events occurred because of deranged, mentally unstable individuals, people who live among us and will continue to do so. Everyone acknowledges that it is impossible to prevent such events from ever happening. The astronomical costs to the detriment of education do not seem to deter bureaucrats from instituting more costly , time-consuming procedures to try to make the schools safer. Shouldn't the total costs, including the ones related to monetary, psychological, and human rights, be taken into account instead of willy nilly implementing draconian procedures like Lock-Down.?

One of these lock-downs occurred while I was a substitute teacher a couple of years ago. I was very grateful there was a teacher assistant who knew what the procedures were. The children were all herded into a little "time out" room at the back of the classroom; the doors were locked, the blinds drawn, all the lights were turned off, and it was our job to keep the students from whispering, even coughing for what seemed like an eternity. We were fortunate that the school in question had been built recently making accommodation for such a hiding facility, something few classrooms have. Altogether the exercise lasted about twenty-five minutes, ruined most of the period, and totally changed the learning atmosphere. It turned out to be merely a Lock-Down drill.

Apparently this practice drill has been instituted in most schools, and is presently being mandated to take place several times a year. I can only say, "Wow!" Does the minute possibility of danger from this source really justify this huge waste of time? If a killer really were stalking the hallways how effective would these measures be? It did not help the students in West Virginia in 2006. The killer went from classroom to classroom looking for his victims, at times shooting through the doors to gain access, killing one heroic teacher in the process.

Reviewing the articles I have gathered as part of my research, I came across six recent media reports involving some Canadian schools and threats of violence. They are as follows: "B.C teachers call for criminal record checks of students." April 30, 2001; "Students shot with pellet gun." September 9, 2006; "School locked down." September 19, 2006; "Written threat found at city school." March 31, 2007; "Alleged school shooting plotter gets lawyer." April 16, 2007; "School threats keep students home." May 1, 2007. (All articles from *Calgary Herald* or *Edmonton Journal*) It would seem school has become much more dangerous recently. I thought the abolition of corporal punishment and the gentle handling of bad behavior was supposed to produce less aggression. Did somebody make a mistake?

Moreover, a new danger has arisen as a result of both procedures instituted to provide safety for Fire Drills and Lock-downs. A letter to the editor in the *Calgary Herald* on September 14, 2006, had the author suggesting that fire drill procedures would directly dovetail with a killer's plans to shoot more people more quickly. Wouldn't having all students congregate in a schoolyard during a fire drill not make for perfect targets for such an individual? In our attempts to be all things to all people we perhaps are leaving ourselves wide open to bigger tragedies. After all, in over fifty years of recorded school history only about 22 people in all of Canada have died as a result of the actions of deranged persons. In light of such miniscule dangers maybe we should re-examine such disruptive and time-wasting practices.

A further aggravation and time waster involves the Intercom. Many teachers complain of the frequent administrative announcements that go on throughout the day. In schools in China and Japan these are strictly prohibited, except perhaps when there is an imminent disaster such as from earthquake tremors. The problem of administrative interruptions could be lessened a great deal with the institution of smaller schools. Smaller schools would probably be beneficial for other problems as well and should be seriously considered for elementary grades. It did not appear to be practical to have small secondary schools in the past, but technology has made many things possible in small, intimate, even home environments. Besides, there are any number of ways to keep announcements to a minimum, especially after classes have begun. Time is our most precious commodity, after life itself, and should not be squandered, especially by administrivia.

Now let's go inside the classroom and examine the time wasters that occur there. The biggest one in my mind is the overuse of audio-visual materials, such as videos, or should I update myself to say Compact Discs. One day in a Senior High School I started the assigned video (from the regular teacher) only to have a girl student groan, "Another video? This is the sixth one we've had today." Had it been my own class I would have immediately changed the lesson, but it was all I had to go on. Many classes include the showing of a video or CD for the entire class period. One year I remember the entire school was bussed to a theatre for viewing a Shakespearean play on the big screen, an exercise that took up the whole afternoon and for which the parents had to pay extra.

Many of these educational audio-visual aids made specially for the classroom feature merely a "talking head", a device which quickly turns off most students. Their attention span lasts all of five minutes. In a darkened, warm classroom it is speculation as to how closely students are involved. And the experts tell us "Don't lecture to the students, if you can help it. Let them discover the concepts by their own efforts." Why do these experts contradict themselves by then recommending the use of videos for the classrooms?

I must admit that a movie presentation seemed like a good idea initially. After all, a theatrical production such as "Macbeth" or "Hamlet" would be much more realistic than dissecting the speeches one by one. Later, as I pondered the amount of teacher and class time this took, I came to the conclusion that this practice is unnecessary, often boring, and a great time-waster. Students could just as easily take the video home for viewing or see it during a noon or free period break. Class time should be spent in active study with a teacher directing the learning. (Memorizing a few lines of Shakespeare wouldn't be such a bad idea either.) Students need a teacher to focus their attention on obscure or meaningful passages or concepts, not just passively watch someone else's presentation. Often I, as the teacher, found it difficult to stay awake during long videos, so I really couldn't blame the students for their inattention. Moreover, we hear the mantra repeatedly that most of us watch too much television or movies anyhow. Extending these same activities into our expensive classrooms makes no sense at all.

Audio-visuals should not take any more than one-third of a period in my opinion. I doubt whether or not such strict guidelines could or should be mandated, but a discussion on this subject would constitute a great talking point for professionals. After all, much has been said and written about getting children away from the television and computer games. Maybe it is time we questioned how this great pacifier is being used in schools. William Coulson, a well-known child psychologist from California, suggests a small child should not watch television for more than one-half hour per day. That limit is perhaps too restrictive for school-age children, but definitely television and movies should have time limits. Expensive and well-equipped schools have many objectives to achieve. Pacifying our children should not be one of them. My advice to parents reading this book is to question their children's teachers to see if he/she uses audio-visuals extensively. Sounds too intrusive? Just remember, it's your child's future you are gambling with, and childhood ends quickly.

Every morning in most modern public schools the copier is going full blast. I used to call this the Copier Waltz, as it hummed along, chung-a-chung-chung. Teachers often come early to get first dibs on the copier for the days' lessons. Many classrooms have shelves and shelves around the room full of photocopied sheets. In the old days when all teachers could use was a mimeograph machine this was hardly possible because it took too many hours of hand labor to prepare, and too much elbow grease to copy. Mostly we used textbooks. The copier was strictly for tests and some special illustrative work. Now most teachers rely constantly on worksheets with paper supplied by the School Board. As a long time conservationist I detest the overuse of unnecessary paper that clogs our landfills and clutters our homes and minds. This kind of overuse has the reverse effect on students despite the trendy use of recycling boxes. It is perhaps not widely known that recycling paper is more expensive than making paper from scratch. I have seen students make one mark on a paper and throw it in the recycling bin thinking they are absolved from blame because it is "recycled". When reminded of how precious, and possibly environmentally destructive, paper is, students seem stunned, and annoyed of course. Our example as educators is not in tune with this admonition when they witness how we overuse it ourselves.

A good part of the reason for this blizzard of paper is because textbook learning is considered a wrongheaded teaching method, and unworthy of a true professional. The true professional makes up lessons out of her/his own resources (read "head" because that's usually what a teacher must rely on in the hurly burly of making up daily lesson plans). In the elementary school, planning lessons means the teacher must create up to eight lesson plans per day, a monumental if not impossible task. In their attempt to fulfill their daily lesson-plan duties teachers resort to many shortcuts usually involving the ubiquitous copy machine. On any school day/week you can usually find teachers collaborating about any "good" lessons they have given to a similar grade, then sharing materials. I am not saying this technique is a bad idea. Quite the contrary ... teacher collaboration has stood the test of time. However, I have seen little attempt to credit the originator or said material or to document the source. This practice gives rise to several questionable educational objectives which were not problems when reputable publishers had their stamp on the assigned textbooks. In the interests of making more time for themselves, teachers have often contravened these conventions.

Moreover, in light of the fact that so many remedial and special classes have been added to educational curriculums, sharing ideas has become very difficult. Even in schools where teachers are involved with identical grades, they are rarely on the same "page" as the other teachers. Normally, lessons dealing with art and perhaps social studies are often shared though the entire school, sometimes becoming a school theme. Good ideas altogether. But for the regular classes the teacher is still left with the monumental task of formulating interesting, meaningful lessons, finding the materials for it in sufficient amount, and writing it down because she/he may be absent the next day due to illness or some unforeseen professional obligation appearing on the time plan. My sympathies extend to High School teachers who must prepare only two or three lessons per day because these lessons, though fewer, are much more complex. I have done both during my teacher career so I know of what I speak. How I longed for the good old standby textbook! I highly suspect most teachers rely on their powers of imagination and spur of the moment ingenuity to get the job done, ... and the mountains of paper piled on shelves ... just in case.

For the substitute teacher the non-use of textbooks has presented special timing difficulties. Realize that the substitute usually receives little notice (perhaps two hours time from morning phone call to arrival at the school). Personally, I was often told that the lesson plan for the day would be arriving shortly. In the 1980's and early 1990's it was necessary for the teacher to get them there by fellow teacher who lived nearby, sometimes by harried husband/wife/partner/roommate who would drop it off on their way to work, and sometimes by special messenger perhaps a taxi. Later in the 1990's and beyond, thanks to electronic mail, these plans would appear on the principal's or secretary's computer. I could just imagine some sick teacher crawling out of bed, dragging herself to the computer to frantically put together something that would be do-able by a complete stranger to her classroom. I do know that many times I entered a classroom to find no evidence of any lesson plans, or something as cursory as "Let the children continue what they were doing yesterday. They know what to do.'

Talk about disaster. I soon learned not to repeat that "lesson plan" to the children or there would immediately commence chaos. If only, if only, I could find the Day Planner, I'd pray. By this thought I refer to the jolly red ring binders, usually issued as a matter of course to every teacher in the schools during the last quarter century, at least in Alberta, British Columbia, and Saskatchewan (speaking from personal experience). When I first started teaching we had to supply our own Day Planners, which I most certainly did. (I'm what is called a Logical-Consequential type person in eduspeak, as opposed to a Random-Abstract, which is what all the "best" teachers wanted to be). I hasten to add, and proudly, that, as a regular teacher, I kept a reasonable record of everything I had taught up to that time, then left a plan for the next few days. Granted these plans, in the days of textbooks for most subjects consisted mainly of pages to be covered, fleshed out with a few details concerning important concepts or special materials that needed to be assembled. How else does one get ready for an unforeseen emergency such as sickness?

When I first started teaching, having a Day Book was a requirement of our professional duties. The Principal explained this to us at our first Orientation meeting of the year . Moreover, we were required to leave this Day Planner on our desks along with the Register of Attendance so that any Principal or Visiting Teacher or Administrator could find it easily, should he/she wish to peruse it in one's absence. During the school day, the teacher could remove these documents to another location, temporarily, if necessary, but they must be produced immediately upon request, and left on the desk for the next day. These were procedures instituted to help teachers and others in the education process provide quick communication among colleagues and, therefore, save Time.

Educators later denigrated these precise instructions as Lock-Step, unimaginative, overly structured, and servile. So, no sense crying about the missing red Daily Planner, just quickly locate the roster of students and the daily agenda of teaching assignments from the Office Even those, on occasion, were missing. Secretaries became one's lifeline, also a handy briefcase containing some classroom material for emergency copying.

I found myself prowling the classroom for those wonderful textbooks, occasionally looking in a few desks of the students at the front of the room, the ones most likely to have some record of what had been under recent study. Yes, dear reader, pressure can drive one to push the bounds of post-modern propriety. You, as a teacher, were considered infringing on a student's privacy by going in a personal desk. My reasoning overcame this objection. These are children for whom I am responsible, albeit for a short time. My children's rooms were their special place, true, but not so special that I or their father could not investigate anytime for any good reason. The sign "Stay Out" does not mean us. After all, they are our responsibility, and therefore, we have our privileges.

I support the dictum that students' desks were never meant to be private from the teachers or administrators of the school; ditto for student lockers. I'm not quite sure when this law appeared, but it certainly put a crimp into school tidiness, (not to mention ability to find illegal or dangerous substances). As an elementary teacher, one of my responsibilities was to inspect and then teach my students how to manage their personal school materials so that they were easily accessible, neatly stacked, and generally in good order. By the early 1980's it became a civil offence to open a student's desk, locker or binder without their personal permission, or a "court order".

I put these words in parenthesis because I really don't know what authority you have to summon, I only know that I as a teacher did not have the authority to do so, on pain of having reprimand up to and including revoking my teaching certificate. *Ipso facto*, classrooms and desks became much messier, aisles were often strewed with backpacks, desks showed little "pride of ownership", and things generally, in the new vernacular, became more "personally imaginative". Meanwhile, trying to cope with messy binders, desks and lockers has become a great time-waster. Add to that a huge and heavy backpack littering the aisles, and classrooms can and have in many cases become a wasteland. Maneuvering around untidy desks, littered backpacks and uncooperative students can and does waste considerable amounts of time.

Getting back to my attempts at finding readily available lessons for the day within fifteen minutes or so, rarely did I find any useful textbooks. Based on the accepted educational guidelines that ".. a true professional doesn't teach for the test, but uses multiple sources for resource material" ... textbooks have almost become obsolete, except perhaps for mathematics and senior sciences. This widely-accepted teaching axiom has evolved and stuck for at least twenty-five years in spite of some highly distasteful results. What, I dare ask, was and is wrong with the use of textbooks by a teacher? Everybody uses books (and now the Internet) to enlarge and enhance their knowledge and to remind them of what needs to be done. Imagine a cook who was not allowed to be use a cookbook, or a lawyer banned from reviewing past judgements, or a manager who was discouraged from planning a budget or writing procedural manuals? To extrapolate this idea even a fraction shows how simple-minded it is. Add to this idiocy, the non-necessity for the same teacher to leave a record of his/her lessons for the subsequent teacher(s) compounds the problem. Textbooks provide a wealth of information and logical sequence as well as sources for their research, relevant illustrations, graphs, maps, glossaries of difficult and new vocabulary, suggestions for further research or study, not to mention the wonderful list of questions provided so that you as the teacher don't spend hours puzzling over how to test the comprehension of your students.

I recall one year I was called upon to introduce a new novel to my Grade Twelve class. The corresponding expectation was that I would also make up the questions (complete with a teacher guide of answers) for subsequent years. I agreed hoping to make Brownie Points, later ruing that day.

As luck would have it I was teaching a total of 105 English students in four different classes, after an absence of several years from the classroom. Much of the curriculum had been changed but not nearly as much as had the marking expectations of students. In the old days day to day questions were answered in class with students revising their answers as we talked. Many quizzes and tests were marked by exchanging papers. Not any more. It soon became apparent that if I wanted good work from my students I would have to mark everything myself. How I dreaded the papers piled on my desk at the end of the day. If these were primary school lessons I could have whizzed through them, because none of the writing assignments had much length, or required serious thought. These major essays by Grade 11 and 12 often took 20 minutes each, multiply that by 105 and you get the idea.

Now where was I going to find the time to read this novel, analyze it and make up interesting and relevant questions while keeping up six and seven classes I taught every day? I searched bookstores for Coles notes (which incidentally are also pooh poohed by teaching experts). Finding none, I bravely started, but finally resorted to hiring someone to finish the job. (Thank you, Bevelyn.) Time and energy were just not on my side. How silly, too, when there are no end of good novels already prepared for teachers, who then can use their time to make the lessons interesting with enough energy left to display some passion for the subject.

This story illustrates just one aspect of the ridiculous notion that the use of textbooks is only for old-fashioned, out-dated drill sergeants who filled the classrooms in days of yore. Textbooks have many virtues, not the least of which is the time saved from preparing lessons. More importantly, everyone, even teachers need a few hours each weekday for personal and family time.

Students must suffer through some time wasters as well. One of these involves the huge binders everyone seems to carry around. They are not necessarily mandated, but seem to be required because of the ubiquitous handouts that must be added daily as they are completed. Young students find this extremely difficult, and older students occasionally delight in opening someone's binder and dumping it. Trying to put it together again can reduce a conscientious student to tears. My experience with teaching has led me to believe that students below the level of senior high school have great difficulty managing a binder and therefore teachers and school policy should devise better arrangements. Grade One and Two should have a single notebook where the students print every lesson, or as much of it as their abilities permit. Teachers can instruct them to print the date at the top, so that can take care of sequence. After Primary school, students can graduate to different workbooks for different subjects, but best not to have them use loose leaf. Keeping ideas in chronological order requires considerable maturity which, by definition, is anathema to young children. Moreover, it requires kids to carry around an awkward ring binder, too large for most backpacks.

As adults we often forget that many of our daily routines have been acquired through countless repetitions. For example, we assume that humans are born with an innate ability to know the English/European system of left to right and top to bottom. If that is the case, how do we explain the Asians who decided to perversely inverse their written language of right to left and bottom to top? In other words, our children must be taught these conventions which takes time and effort on the part of both teachers and students. Expecting children to know how to arrange and manage a large amount of individual sheets of paper is asking a lot. By October, most student binders up to Grade Eight begin to look like wastebaskets. I know I have spent precious class-time minutes trying to help a student to locate some material in their binder, mostly to give up because it was taking too much time. I think we should we devise a more efficient method or return to the bound scribblers that were used in the past.

The argument of homework for students has evoked considerable argument of late. After careful evaluation, I am on the negative side. No homework up to Grade 6 at least, except perhaps for special school projects, and not on a regular basis. After that, homework should be limited to studying for exams, reviewing lessons, extra reading and catching up on missed school work. If a student has homework every day there is something wrong with their work habits at school. Parents should question this. This constitutes more regulated time, and our lives are already overfull of these activities.
In addition, textbooks and workbooks should remain in the classroom for most of the time. I disagree with Andrew Nikiforuk, a leading expert on education, and others that say all students should have homework. Homework is a great timewaster for children and parents

alike. Evenings should be family time, not parents riding herd on their offspring policing the work assigned by a teacher. The leading article in *Maclean's Magazine,* August, 2006, entitled "Homework is killing our kids" shows a truly heart-wrenching picture of a young girl head down on her homework. That photo sums up my feelings about homework. Too much! Too much! Maybe students would work better during school hours if they could not use the argument that "I'll do it for homework". My critics would counter-argue that Canadian education is far less onerous for time than in some countries where school takes up the whole day from 8 a.m. to 6 p.m. My rebuttal includes that in these countries, the school days are interspersed with active play every hour. Moreover, many of those schools take on a much greater range of education than our schools do, including music, the arts, and apprenticeship training.

Another newspaper article regarding homework appeared in the *Calgary Herald,* September 6, 2007, which reviewed a recent book written by retired teacher and author, Vera Goodman, entitled *Simply Too Much Homework!* Another article talks about " ..Homework is creating stress in the home... " (*Calgary Herald,* October 15, 2006) It seems my feelings are shared by other conscientious Canadian teachers and parents.

Begging the reader's indulgence I wish to bring up one small, but irritating feature regarding the few textbooks that do appear in classrooms. Every few years these textbooks seemed to undergo revisions and School Board were required to purchase new ones. Besides adding to the expense of education, the general guideline seems to be to make these textbooks as large and cumbersome as possible. I guess a regular seven inch by ten inch textbook does little to challenge a seventh grader who must stuff it into his backpack. How much more challenging (and I guess educational) it will be for him to find room for the fourteen by twenty inch textbook, push it into his backpack along with his two huge binders, an extra large pencil case, his Walkman, his water bottle, his gym strip and runners, a ruler, his leftover lunch, etc. My sympathies extend to these poor overburdened wretches as they pack up, even if Charlie has been the class clown for the three periods and made your life miserable with his antics.

I guess backpacks are here to stay, but I want parents to be aware they have proven to be, if not time wasters, then aggravation causers. Students lug them into school and dump them unceremoniously into the aisles. The bigness of the backpack seems to be inversely proportional to the seriousness of the student. I swear the most positive aspect of many backpacks must be credited to promoting the strong backs and tough biceps which students develop from carrying them to, from, and around in school. I cringe at the idea of coming down hard on all those backpacks, but I really caution parents to be wary of children carrying too much weight in them. Secretly I think it would be wonderful if backpacks became a thing of the past. Someday maybe my grandchildren will thank me.

The Semester System for senior high school should also be re-examined for its shortcomings particularly in the matter of wasting time. When students spent a whole year on a variety of subjects, they wrote larger tests only twice per year, before Christmas and again in June. Classes were shut down at those times and exams were held in a matter of a week for the midterms, and a couple of weeks for the final, departmental exams in June. Now that most schools have adopted the semester system the first semester is severely restricted as to Time because of the impending Christmas vacation when school personnel become restless in anticipation. After the holiday, Alberta students return to classes very briefly, and immediately go into the exam mode. Not much can be taught or learned in that brief period, so the whole of January is basically a non-teaching month. Teachers, then, are often "seconded" to go to Edmonton to mark the departmental exams, which means students often start the next semester with a substitute teacher. They barely get started when classes are again interrupted for two days of Teachers' Convention, then one day of Family

Appreciation Day, a five-day weekend. Furthermore, many classes, such as Second Language learning, do not lend themselves well to constricted time allotments. Most people learn much better when exposed to new concepts over an extended period of time. If more choice was allowed for school choice we could compare the results of the two systems, and decide on the basis of that experiment which one we wish our children to attend.

Swim Lessons during School Time

I know I'm going to sound like a Grinch on this one, but I fail to see how the public can justify spending funds on teachers, buses, bus drivers, and swimming instructors where a whole school takes the morning or afternoon off while the students are taught how to swim. I have personally experienced many school half days where ten teachers sit up in the stands watching 60 or 70 students splash around in the water. True, the swim instructors seem to be fun people and the kids seem to enjoy it, but why should it take place during school time? In today's culture many of these children are given swimming lessons by their parents already. Many districts have swimming pools and residents are required to pay fees as members of that community. Many more families spend time at summer resorts which regularly conduct swimming lessons. Very few children in our modern cities do not have access to affordable swimming lessons and pool time. Therefore, having elementary students take swimming lessons during school time is a great Time, education, and money waster in my opinion.

I can hear the rebuttal loud and clear. Students are not forced to take these lessons which, by the way, must be paid for extra by the parents. Those who opt out of the lessons can stay behind in the school with teacher supervision. Moreover, if the swimming fee is a problem you can apply to the administration for charity.

All of these options leave much to be desired. Firstly, most parents do not want to humiliate themselves by asking for charity, so they dig deep cutting out the possible trip to the zoo, or other excursion. Secondly, children left behind are usually sent to the library or to a common classroom with other stay-behinds. They must face the humiliation of being different and left out as well as missing regular teacher instruction, often being bored with their own company. It is a waste of time for teachers to conduct regular classes because only a few of the students are left behind. During this time, school is not a fun place to be for a young child whose self esteem, to use a modern catch phrase, is undergoing a severe testing.

Okay, okay, so I am a Grinch. But wouldn't it make more sense to have the swim classes scheduled for after school where a bus could deliver the children to the nearest swimming pool under the supervision of a few volunteer parents or grandparents, or possibly even a paid supervisor? The teachers would not be affected, regular classes would not be affected, parents and children would be freer to state and pay for their own choice of activity, and most important, school time would not be wasted. Maybe it makes too much sense. Maybe it has been done in the past and we don't want to upset the old applecart. Maybe teachers like to get out of a morning or afternoon of teaching. Maybe all of the above. This practice has gone on since the 1980's and shows no sign of stopping in most of the elementary schools in Calgary. I have never heard one word of protest against it, so I guess I'm the only one who finds it objectionable.

You think?

CHAPTER FIVE – LOW PUBLIC ACCOUNTABILITY

"American public education suddenly went into a tailspin in the middle 1960's. That tailspin coincided with the rapid centralization of public education away from parental control and local accountability, and into the hands of state and federal bureaucracies."

Warren T. Brookes, Syndicated Columnist, *Detroit News*

Over the years, taxpayers and even parents have been if not eliminated from the education process in meaningful ways, at least sidelined to such and extent that their voices are muted at best. This situation has devolved over the years from a model geared to local control, directly answerable to the consumers of the product, namely the parents whose children attend the school and the taxpayers who pay for it.

Originally, the ratepayers of a small school district of approximately 36 square miles, met to discuss how to set up a local school. My father told us a few of the details from the rural district of Devonshire where he was one of the original Board members before he had any children of his own. The School District received a small grant from the provincial government indicating the land that had been set aside and some specifications for how a schoolhouse should be built. Most of the labor for construction was done by volunteers, which occurred after seeding and before harvest.

The construction completed, a School Board was chosen mostly through a process of recruitment, but, if more than the five to seven required were anxious to serve, a vote would be taken. None of these positions paid any salary. The Local School Board then chose a Chairman from amongst their members and proceeded to find and interview a teacher. The teacher normally lived with one of the Board members until such time as a two-room Teacherage could be built. The teacher then walked to work early enough to start the wood stove so that the room would be warm enough for pencils to be used. He/she was also responsible for the care-taking and cleaning duties in the school and students were expected to help. Most students willingly participated in their turn as blackboard monitor, water carrier, book tidying, even desk washing et cetera, on a rotating basis. I understand many Japanese and Chinese students still do all or most of the caretaking duties for their classrooms.

Many logistical difficulties had to be solved. This was a time when families were very large so that a teacher might be handling many students. I recall a speech by our Superintendent in about 1965 who informed us newly-minted teachers that his first school consisted of eighty students. Textbooks were few and expensive, but were generally mandated and supplied by the district or the provincial government. Students/parents purchased their own notebooks (scribblers, we called them) and writing supplies, usually through the school at a bulk price. I do not remember a charge for textbook rental until I got into High School, but textbooks were carefully scrutinized by the teacher at the beginning and end of each school year to determine if their condition was good enough to be used again. Various admonitions occurred during the year to encourage students not to abuse their textbooks. Most lessons were taught orally by the teacher with a few notes copied from the chalkboard (which was called the blackboard because of its color). Older students often made notes from information in the textbooks. The only copy machine was a jelly-covered flat where the teacher could laboriously copy one sheet at a time after making a master ink copy. In my first year of teaching I still used one of these getting ink-stained hands as a reward.

As you can imagine, the wishes and expectations of the local people at this time were front and centre at all times. For example, everyone looked forward to the ubiquitous Christmas Concert which the teacher was required to organize for the parents and neighbors. Her (occasionally his) budget for this extravaganza was meager if indeed it existed at all. I can recall it as a magical night filled with fumes from the dangerous gas lamps lit especially for the occasion. Eaton's company graciously supplied small gifts for all the pre-school children and the children in school picked names for gift exchange. We each received a small paper bag of candies and nuts together with one, precious Japanese orange.

Quite a difference now exists in the sixty years hence. Schools are now swimming in paper, art supplies, copiers, and books. A few schools still put on the Christmas concert, but it is not mandatory, and certainly not every teacher is required to take part. In the past, the teacher was visited once or twice per year by the Provincial Superintendent to check up on the progress of the students and the efficiency of the teacher. Waste was considered as bad a trait as theft certainly when it concerned actual dollars being spent. Those were the old days when public money was heavily scrutinized, much like the scrutiny awarded a sacred trust.

Most of today's teachers would find such work conditions overly stressful, and I agree that many of these large expectations are not necessary in our changed circumstances. However, we could not have imagined the extreme attitude of entitlement that pervades our society at present. Citizens, whether they pay taxes or not, make huge demands on the public purse. These demands extend to education, second only to Health Care. Knowing that Canadians presently pay approximately 45% (2007) of what they earn to support the various levels of government, we should be very concerned about how these dollars are spent.

Canada is the top spender in public education according to the Fraser Institute. Originally, it cost ten dollars per year to educate a child, which would translate into approximately five hundred dollars today, factoring in inflation since then. Last year's budget, 2005, the comparable figure was pegged at approximately $8770.00 per regular student. Amounts for students with special needs easily reached $20,000.00. Has there been a corresponding increase in how well students are being educated? Evidence suggests not by a long shot.

As early as 1950, many American families realized something was wrong "We had the most expensive educational system in the history of civilization; yet, it was graduating many young people who could not spell, write a correct sentence, work simple arithmetic, or read with understanding; who had not been disciplined in work habits: who were ignorant of the history and traditions of their own country." . (*Dan Smoot Report*, Texas, Oct.1966) Much of the blame must be laid at the feet of the new "progressive model" of education because most American schools had adopted these ideas by 1935 thanks in large part to the efforts of Mr. John Dewey. He had been preaching his ideas to prospective teachers as head of Teachers College at Columbia University since 1904 until his retirement in 1930. I contrast these dates with Canada's public education history which lagged about ten years later, starting in Eastern Canada and filtering westward.

My own concerns regarding the efficacy of these directions and goals started while I was teaching Grade One in 1959. At that time, I had a *Teacher's Guide* for the Dick and Jane reading series that read like a drama script. We were cautioned to try to use it word for word as it was written. "Follow the *Guide*. Don't second guess the experts." It was my first year of teaching, so I tried to follow these instructions to the letter. Several of the students could not seem to grasp the instructions and seemed to be very slow to learn by rote from the flash cards. I voiced my concerns to my more experienced colleagues most of whom repeated the same advice. In that year a supervising teacher chastised me for using some phonics rather than the set procedure which made me aware of how much importance they attached to these instructions. These were experts while I was a novice. Ten years later, my concerns seemed to be confirmed as I read widely and tried to get information from many different sources.

One would think that such revelations would resonate with educational authorities across Canada. I naively believed, that, once known, immediate steps would be taken to ameliorate the situation or, better, to reverse the process and return to the tried and true methods, at least until these revolutionary ideas could be proven to work better than the traditional ones. Unfortunately, this did not happen. It appeared that the education establishment in the halls of higher learning were fully committed to the Dewey's principles and determined to push ahead. Critics of the established order were dismissed as outdated fearmongers, ignorant of the true worth of progressive education. It would merely take more time to prove how superior these new methods were.

There seemed to be a temporary reversal in the American approach to education after the Soviet Union launched Sputnik in 1957, but again these policies were reversed in favor of progressivism under the presidencies of Kennedy and Johnson. Since then, the platforms of the Democratic Party in United States have consistently favored government interference in education while ignoring the wishes of parents. Canadian education tended to follow along slavishly, which I find very puzzling in light of Canada's antipathy to most things American. Granted, most of these criticisms consist mainly of verbal statements. Our actions belie our words, certainly in most aspects of education.

In the years since, many studies confirmed the earlier warnings about the effects of progressive education over the long term. A comprehensive study by the Southam newspaper chain was conducted in 1987 covering both Canada and United States. As near as I can ascertain, they tried to be as objective in their findings as empirical science demands. The *Southam Literacy Report* used interviews from 2,398 adults in 148 Canadian communities and rural areas, drawing from a random cross-section of the entire population.

"An average interview took 80 minutes and involved two parts: a background and activity questionnaire followed by a test of reading, writing and numbers skills using 61 items based on everyday life. These literacy items were adapted from a 1985 U.S. survey for the National Assessment of Educational Progress by substituting Canadian spellings, materials and topical references.

"The standards for literacy were determined by a 25-member panel drawn from al walks of life." (*Calgary Herald*, September 12, 1987).

Incidentally, Canada's literacy rate is listed as 98% in the World Almanac, which shows us how unreliable are the figures contained in that publication.

The results of illiteracy rates were astounding as follows:
72% of students Grade 4 and under (poor, but possibly understandable)
24 % of high school dropouts (what?)
24% of Canadians overall
17% of High School graduates
13% of University dropouts
11% pf Community college or trade school students
8 % of University Graduates

You may well ask, "How can somebody graduate from university and still be classed as illiterate?" I have my suspicions, but will leave that for someone else to answer.

These numbers amounted to 4.5 million illiterates in Canada, most of whom had attended at least ten years of school since school is compulsory up until a child is fifteen years old. I contrast these statistics with my father's situation. He attended school for only three years before the turn of the twentieth century using only a slate, phonics, and the old rote learning, teacher-directed system yet was able to read our university tests. Because of pioneer conditions with few or no veterinarians, he also compelled himself to read about, understand, and carry out complicated animal husbandry techniques using the Book. I well remember the huge tome he hauled out time again to try to solve a disease condition of one of the farm animals. He (as well as my mother, but she was a Grade 8 graduate so it was expected of her) was an avid reader throughout his life despite the difficulty and scarcity of getting reading material. His school experience was similar to many of the second genration pioneers, who all seemed to be able to read adult publications and do elementary math without calculators or other devices.

The statistics from the Southam report were comparable for Americans as well as Canadians. My immediate thought was, "Now, finally they (meaning the Education Establishment of government leaders and teachers' unions) will do something to correct this failure to provide what they are being paid to do. Has it happened in the interim? It doesn't appear so. A recent newspaper report in 2006 mentioned that the illiterate numbers are about the same while a full 40% of Canadians are lacking the necessary literacy and numeracy skills to fully function in today's highly technological society. (<u>Calgary Herald-N13</u>, September 14, 2006. Alex Fraser-Harrison)

Some steps by other groups have been undertaken in attempts to correct this appalling state of affairs. Albertans for Quality Education was organized and held several conferences to discuss the situation and suggest some options for parents. Literacy Alberta is a similar non-profit organization dedicated to promoting literacy. Several educational companies focusing on traditional basic skills have come into existence, such as the Sylvan Learning System centers, Oxford Learning Centres, Kumon Math – recently expanded to Kumon Reading as well, and The Academy of Math and Science to name a few. The yellow pages in the Calgary telephone book contains at least four full pages of similar private businesses dealing with elementary and secondary education. Many families are urged to "school proof" their young children, meaning don't count on the schools to teach your child the basics of reading and writing in either official language and mastering simple arithmetic. I have met several adults, graduates of years of public education who have serious literacy problems, but are too ashamed to discuss it openly or get help for their problem. The public education system should be held accountable for these results.

Home-schooling has become a way of life for many families, mostly, it seems, for homes with strong Christian beliefs. They are proving very effective in educating their children despite the poor "funding" they receive. In effect, they receive no dollars plus must purchase all their own materials. Add to this that few of these parents are trained in the teaching skills yet still manage to educate their children to university level. Their attempts have been rewarded when many of their students have attained scholarships for post-secondary institutions. In fact, many prestigious post-secondary institutions now welcome if not recruit graduates from home-schooling. In spite of these successes, " The teachers' unions would love to shut down home-schoolers" says a report in a local newspaper. (*Calgary Herald,* December 8, 2006, by J. Woodward) In 2007 Alberta Learning reported that there were some 10,000 home-schooled children which represened two percent of school-age kids. It seems ironic that, despite the success of home-schoolers, governments demand that home-schooled children must be enrolled in and affiliated with a properly approved Public School Board, and be inspected by that Board. I question who are the REAL experts in the field?

Another new development along these lines has been the emergence of Charter Schools, a spin-off from similar steps taken in the United States. There are six Charter Schools in Calgary at present, with more in the planning stages. It displeases me to realize each of these educational movements were forced by provincial legislators to apply first through the local Public School Boards with mostly negative results. Only then could they apply to another, more friendly Public School Board or to the provincial government directly, in their attempts to access some of the public funds. This fact illustrates how suspicious of local control our governments are, and how much they trust the perspicacity, or perhaps fear the animosity, of the powerful teachers' unions and educational bureaucrats.

I was briefly involved with one of these charter school attempts and so have some knowledge of the enormous time, research, expertise, and money it took to establish a charter school, and the negativity projecting from the public school system. In light of this attitude, I could not help wondering whether the education of our young people was actually the primary concern of our provincial government, which is the final arbiter of what passes as educational standards in each province.

A most sensible approach was suggested by Milton Friedman, a Nobel prize winner in economics in 1976. He proposed that every child of school age be given an educational voucher in trust to the parents to be used exclusively for the educational institution of their choice. The idea appeared to be a "no brainer" ... what a wonderful idea! You would think that serious educators would be ecstatic. Educational institutions should have a HUGE advantage since they were already established and well known. Not so fast. Nothing has become so distasteful to these educational experts. One scarcely sees or hears it mentioned. I find it occasionally on the Letters to the Editor page, or mentioned on Talk Radio, but it is a poisonous subject it seems for anyone in the Field so has been relegated to the Trash Heap of Genuinely Good & Innovative Ideas, (especially if these ideas verge into the area of a free marketplace for the business of Education).

Further measures have been implemented in the past by the same educrats to contradict, obscure or hide the evidence of serious deficiencies in the present system. I cannot think of any of these objectives which caused as many problems as the question of whether or not to continue with external testing of educational results. Who can fail to realize that having students tested is fundamental to Educational Accountability? If all education was taken care of by the private sector, poor results would soon find those schools with a freefall in student enrollment. However, in a mandatory, publicly-funded system, how else do you keep the system honest?

The Educational Establishment disagreed. They argued if teachers were properly trained both before and during their working lives there would be no need for outside testing. In the late 1970's this objective was discussed extensively in several of the teacher conferences which I attended. At least five "professional days during the school year" for teachers became a mantra along with the need for teachers to obtain a Bachelor of Education degree. At that time there still were many older teachers who had started to teach with a single year of training sometimes supplemented by Summer School classes, exactly the route I had followed. The rationale was that once an individual had obtained a university degree, it was disrespectful of the public to question their professionalism by outside tests, marked by others. Therefore, teachers' groups led the fight to eliminate outside testing for public school students, directly affecting approximately ninety percent of the the school population at that time. This objective succeeded in most of the provinces in Canada at least for a few years. In Alberta the lack of Grade 12 Final Exams lasted from about 1977 to 1985. Other provinces are even less accountable which we will go into later.

In my experience, the only saving grace for this audacious experiment was that, in Alberta at least, the alarming consequences became evident very soon afterward. In bureaucratic terms, this means within ten years, too long a time when one considers a school lifetime for most kids is only ten or twelve years. Post secondary institutions wailed that they had no way of ascertaining whether these High School graduates were competent to be enrolled. Marks by individual teachers ranged widely in assessing competence. Businesses were loathe to hire these young people for anything but the most entry level jobs, and were forced to train them from scratch. Post secondary institutions instituted entrance level exams, and then set up remedial classes. My daughter was one of those forced to take what I would call a high school composition class where she wrote her essays during class. She could not do this outside of class time because by then computers were becoming prevalent and "entrepreneurs" had figured out how to sell plagiarized essays. All of these innovations were costing institutions time and money.

Finally, governments were forced to listen. Subsequently, Alberta adopted the policy whereby Grade 12 diploma was granted after a student attained 100 credits for classes taken, passed each of those with a minimum of 50%, plus had taken and passed exams in five core subjects, instituted and marked by the provincial Department of Education. The core subjects were made up of two English exams (one essay type and one multiple choice), a senior level Social Studies exam, one Senior science exam, and one Senior math exam. The results from these exams count for 50%, the teacher's mark for the other 50%, a bare minimum in my opinion. Add to this scenario that both English and Social Studies have lower level or non-academic classes as a choice for its students and you get the picture of perhaps why graduates are really not as well educated as their peers from forty or fifty years ago on the average.

Each province has different expectations and examinations for their High School graduates. I found it very difficult to get this information by searching web sites, so if you are moving from one province to another it is best to get the information early, probably by asking the principal of a local high school. Consequently, it must be a headache for institutions of higher learning as well as businesses that are looking to hire these people. Simplification and streamlining throughout the entire country would be much appreciated by parents and students alike I am sure.

If Alberta standards appear to be somewhat low, other provinces appear to be even less demanding. In Saskatchewan, no departmental exams need to be taken if the teacher is accredited. Accreditation is granted if the teacher has a professional degree plus has attended one or two seminars on government directives and initiatives in education, not terribly rigorous from the aspect of accountability. I am personally acquainted with teachers there who became accredited. Naturally, there are many exceptional and conscientious teachers who do their best, but I would not go so far as to trust them completely in evaluating my child's competence to embark on post-secondary education or job hunting.

If the teacher is not accredited, students write departmental exams, but only 40% of these marks are counted toward the student's final grade; the other 60% comes from the classroom teacher.

I recall only one experience where I was faced with giving Grade 12 students their final grade mark. As the end of the year approached I found myself approached several times by students and sometimes even parents who were trying to persuade me to be generous with final marks. Need I add, that these usually involved students who had not put out the effort normally expected of them. Several times I felt very uncomfortable and tried, diplomatically, to avert the final decision. Tensions became more strained as June approached. As luck would have it, the teachers went on strike during the month of June so I was spared the pain of the final few days, although I did have to decide on those final marks. After that experience, it seemed incongruous to me that any teacher would object to having someone or some other authority take this burden off their shoulders.

Up until about 1970, all senior matriculants had to write every final exam and received 100% of their final mark from this source. My own experience followed this scenario, and although writing the whole set of final exams was traumatic it was also satisfying when you succeeded. As a young person from rural Saskatchewan, I immediately knew somewhat where I stood in relation to all the other young people whom I encountered later. Everyone of us had had to endure this debut establishing some true self-esteem as a result. In retrospect, final exams became realistic way of determining your education status among your peers.

Alberta also re-introduced standardized testing for some of the earlier grades as well, despite the howls of protest by the teachers' unions and much of the media spin. You may not be aware, however, that students can be exempted from these tests if the parent or teacher recommends it. I disagree. Every student should be required to take these tests so that results will not be skewed in one direction or another. Despite the objectives of some sectors, results of the standardized tests have become a popular item every spring in Western Canada. The Fraser Institute from Vancouver now publishes a newspaper report on how each school in British Columbia, Alberta, and Saskatchewan has performed on these tests. They also audaciously rank the schools according to these results. Now parents eagerly await these reports so as to ascertain how "their" school is doing and where they are in the hierarchy. Critics mourn that all this ranking is so demeaning, but human nature demands this be done, whether we face it openly, or whisper it quietly via the grapevine.

The B.C. Teachers' Union consistently downplays and disparages these results, as does the Alberta Teachers' Union, saying " .. the Institute is merely shilling for privatization of schools…" (*Alberta Report*, April 1, 2002) They also insist that private schools discriminate against children from "disadvantaged families", so far a purely hypothetical argument. The question that comes to mind is why do they so dislike the idea of accountability? If the public education system is so superior, they should welcome any and all comparisons.

Anastasios Kotsikonas expressed it this way in a paper written in 1991/92 entitled "Discussion on Policies and Practices in Canadian Institutions".

> "Once again, it would seem that we as educators are more interested in engaging in the practice of navel gazing (rather) than seeking to understand the basis for why governments and the public demand a quantitative accounting for what goes on in schools."

In summary, I now quote some horror stories related to the lack of accountability in schools.

1. "St Joe students not ready for exams." " About half of the Grade 12 students will not write their English diploma exams this year after the school adopted a self-paced learning program. (*Edmonton Journal*, June 6, 1999)
2. " .. a large percentage of teachers represent the very bottom of the academic achievement barrel, and as such, fall easy prey to mindless and destructive fads." (Walter E. Williams, *Western Standard*, March 29, 2004)

3. "Classification Test of verbal analogy and elementary arithmetical computations, the teachers scored, on average, only slightly better than clerical workers." (same article as #2)
4. "..science professors Milwood Motley and Larry Williams (were fired), both of whom refused to go along with the college's Success Equals Effort (SEE) policy. SEE is a policy where 60 percent of a freshman's grade is based on effort and the rest on academic performance." (Williams, *Western Standard*, November 8, 2004)
5. "Geography quiz shows one in 10 (American students) can't even locate U.S. without help." Canada and Mexico were included in this survey as well as several European countries. Canada performed somewhat better than both the U.S. and Mexico, but John Fahey, president of the National Geographic Society said, "..the simple lack of geographic knowledge (indicates) the apparent retreat of young people from a global society in an era that doesn't allow such luxury." (Paul Recer in The *Maui News*, November 21, 2002. i.e. post 9-11)
6. President of the Alberta Teachers' Association said that rather than read the Fraser Institute Report on school rankings, it was better for parents to ".. go into the schools and look in children's faces .." (Rutherford Radio Show, AM770, January 31, 2006)
7. Teachers, Principals, and parents can "opt out" some students from the standardized tests for Grades 3, 6, and 9 for any reason whatever. This puts into doubt the big question of how accurate are the published results.
8. The stated purpose of the Calgary Board of Education is to "Ensure individual Student Development Through Effective Education." This statement is so vague as to be useless in determining whether the schools are delivering a good education to their customers. (CBE brochure, 2006-2007)

Report Cards deserve a mention at this stage. Many of us recall with happy nostalgia the old report cards from schools where children were given number grades from 0 to 100 for different subjects. Moreover, the subjects listed were rarely more than eight.... Language, Reading or Literature, Science or Biology, Chemistry, or Physics (depending on grade level), Arithmetic or Mathematics or Algebra, the ubiquitous Social Studies, Health, maybe Music or Art Appreciation, later Physical Education, and several others. Any parent could readily grasp what was being evaluated, and consequently whether they were doing well, average, or poorly. Students knew quite specifically where they stood in relation to where they should be. As well, an increase in one or two marks from one reporting period to the next was significant and an excellent tool for a teacher to indicated even a little extra effort. That is what a Report Card is supposed to accomplish, I had always assumed. Parents of today's young children are either bemused or puzzled by today's report cards, ever since about 1980. Each subject can have as many as 5, 10, 15, even 17 different marks, usually with a letter grade of A, B, C or !, 2, 3 plus teacher comments. I pity the poor teachers who have to complete these reports as well. What does it all mean? I seriously wonder whether they are designed to confuse rather than give parents and understanding of what a child is actually accomplishing in school.

I recently received a report from colleague who attended the vaunted Swedish school, often considered a Utopia to be emulated by Canadians and other progressive countries. The report is entitled "The Terrible Effects of Public Schooling". I quote from his report:

- " ..another myth of the Swedish socialist supremacy was revealed to be completely untrue..... After having spent nine mandatory years in school, 11.4% of Swedish children don't meet the requirement to go to high school.
- "...Also, the requirements to go to high school are set on such an absurdly low level that no one should be able not to make it.
- "...For starters, in the requirement only three subjects actually count: mathematics, Swedish, and English.... and you need a "pass" in all three...

- "… there are only three "grades": pass, pass with distinction, and pass with even more distinction…
- "…the only way to not meet the requirement …is intended for those youngsters who never bother to show up (which is only possible if you manage to stay away from your parents, school teachers, as well as the police, since not being in school is a crime)." (e-mail from Alar Aksberg, 2007)

I include this example to show how ridiculous standards can become when we attempt to be nice to every child, never letting them experience the trauma of failing, of being judged in comparison to their peers. In effect, we are endeavoring to defy human nature.

Education may be a special kind of business, but it is still a business because it answers a basic human need. As a business there must be accountability as well as openness. Our clients are so immature that they can easily be influenced or manipulated, which demands even more scrutiny. It is a wonder that parents seem so easily persuaded to accept the *status quo* without question. Maybe it is time to have another look.

CHAPTER SIX – PRESSURE GROUPS

"We have become so democratic in our habits of thought that we are convinced that truth is determined through a plebiscite of facts."

Joseph Heller, c1975

Public School has become a seething cauldron of pressure groups seeking to advance their agendas through this compulsory agency. So much so that the original purpose of school which was to give every child a basic academic foundation in written and numeracy arts, and a understanding of where we have come from so that we may know where we are heading, has been largely backed into an obscure corner. All of these pressure groups are ultimately sure that they have a most important message that simply MUST be addressed if children can (1) be made safer (2) be made aware of world-shaking information (3) be able to live in our modern world (4) come up to speed in tolerance and understanding, et cetera. I daresay a teacher or parent from 100 years ago would be completely puzzled as to what was going on if he or she dropped into one of our modern schools. The question would probably be, "When do the regular school lessons begin?"

The following are some of the pressure groups which have made significant inroads and managed to inculcate their pet projects onto the education stream:

1. <u>Sex Education</u> – starting now earlier and earlier, certainly by Grade Four, children are taught about changes in body structures, hormones, and functions for boys and girls. Experts are brought in, films are shown, and open questions are answered presumably

because parents won't give their offspring the proper information. In recent years the discussion on homosexuality, lesbianism, and bi-sexualism comes front and center along with the exhortation that sexual orientation is a personal choice, and no one choice is any better that any other. Sadly, the general impression that young minds absorb is that these aberrant choices are more "sexy", more up-to-date than the "old, outdated" approach to sex. This message occurs before children have any basis on which to decide about these important life choices. The Abstinence Movement has tried to make inroads onto this scene, but have largely been sidelined, ignored, or refused time allotments to share their message. Informal observation seems to indicate that whenever a Sex Education program has occurred there is a requisite increase in sexual activity by the student body, sometimes with several young girls getting pregnant.

If one examines the history of this movement to liberalize sex among teenagers, it appears to have started in the mid 1970's as part of the sexual revolution going strong at the time. Previously, criminal charges could be applied to the seducer of any girl under the age of 18. The push for lowering the "Age of Consent" was a major project for several members of Parliament through the late 1970's and 1980's. Finally, in 1988, Amendments to the *Criminal Code* set the age of consent at 14 years old for both girls and boys. So little fanfare accompanied this massive change to sexual rights for children that most Canadians were unaware of its existence until hearing a news report about a 14 or 15 year-old unmarried girl who won the right to keep her baby over the objections of her parents. I recall one where the parents wanted her to give it up for adoption, another where they did not want her to have an abortion. Both times the court ruled in favor of the child. I must admit that I was among the millions of Canadians who remained ignorant of this law at the time.

The new sex rights for children, fostered and promoted in schools, have had terrible consequences for parents and families. Fourteen year olds have now the power to overrule parents in terms of who they wish to "date" and how they wish to deal with its consequences, up to and including a child or children that this behavior produces. The general public may not be aware of a program in Alberta, often referred to as the "Jimmy Program", which provided funding for any child, 16 and over, who found their home conditions "intolerable". It appeared to me that many simply used this program as a way to live on their own. Clandestine stories could be overheard in the schools about gang bang parties held in these apartments and boyfriends coming and going at all hours of the day and night. A good cry in front of a counselor could usually produce the desired result. "My mother, or dad, hates me. He/she/they yell at me." If that didn't work, you could always add, "My stepdad, my mom's boyfriend, my uncle tries to touch me on my private parts." Seldom were the parents consulted before public services took over.

2. <u>Special Programs for Pregnant Girls</u> – have been implemented in many school districts, usually spearheaded by a compassionate, caring woman who was appalled by the public censure and family embarrassment received by unmarried, pregnant girls up to that time. Not content with simply special programs in a separate school building, these girls now usually enjoy the benefit of daycare centres for their offspring and special counselors to tell them how much it isn't their fault, all at public expense. They are absolved from any guilt or even bad feeling about what they have done. It is as if they have have had no hand in this "happening".

Naturally, special academic programs must be created for each as an individual because they are in different grades and have different levels of education, plus they enter the facility at odd times of the year. I have been in a several of these schools over the years and have found the girls happily comparing baby pictures or celebrating the birth of the newborn baby and its child mother complete with party favors, cake, and presents. Very seldom was the option of adoption even considered.

How different from when I was young. Unwed pregnancy was the worst thing that could befall a young girl at a time when birth control was based purely on monthly time management, a very unsatisfactory method at best. It followed that abstinence was the only safe option. Yes, a few girls did make "mistakes" and were usually ushered into a quick marriage, or went to visit Aunt Gladys in a city far away. Maybe these were rather severe consequences, but having a child out of wedlock, being raised by a single mother who has a poor education and few prospects of making a decent living is not a sterling option for the child in question. Single motherhood is now almost a mark of martyrdom, and Dads as part of the family are never taken for granted. Schools must cope with the problems of possible abductions by absentee parents, and carefully screen anyone who comes to transport a child from school. None of these consequences were considered before our rush to sexual freedom of expression. Schools have promoted these values, both overtly, but subtly through celebrating child parenthood, and sex education. The true cost of these new values has yet to be paid.

3. <u>Environmental Groups</u> – from Carmanah to Brazil's Rain Forests, to Ban DDT, to Save the Grizzlies', or the Whales, or the Wolves, and beyond, there is never a lack of topics for these projects. Each special-interest group requests to have their time in the classroom, and many of them have succeeded. Young people are told over and over again until they are convinced that they are the Idealists, and the adults are merely jaded, outdated, and stingy with their money. Many impressionable young minds absorb these platitudes and often go overboard in pursuit of them. Rarely do students hear the opposing arguments at the same time. School administrators will

tell you that children are very computer literate and have access to computers, which is true. However, a personal presentation by a convert or the classroom teacher is much more powerful than anything one can read off a website. Moreover, how many of us actually remember a topic long enough to research it thoroughly? Very few, and usually they represent mature adults. In public schools, with a captive audience, it is fairly easy to warp young minds (especially if that is your intent). Moreover, most of these projects involve money, therefore they can wait until students are on their own before they decide to put money and effort into any such special promotions.

I suppose the argument could be made that students should be made aware of environmental concerns, but I would caution that such projects should be left to post-secondary institutions, or at least high school with proponents of both sides having their say in close proximity to each other, if the time and personnel are available and the subject fits in with a regular subject studied. Seldom do these conditions exist. In other words, students should be exposed to a real dialectic. If neither time nor opportunity allows, the best solution, then, is probably to keep such projects out of the schools and concentrate on the basics of the subject at hand.

4. <u>Rights of the Child</u> - Spearheaded by the United Nations, this movement started with good intentions, so it seems. To quote Ted Byfield in the *Calgary Sun*, November 21, 1999, "It begins as a good and noble cause -- and then it just goes nuts." During the 1980's we learned that child sweatshops existed in many parts of the Third World. Children spent twelve or fourteen hours in isolated rooms without windows while their nimble fingers were busy making carpets, or ornaments, or any number of consumer goods for sale to the Developed World. One atrocious fact I recall was that Michael Jordan ~~Shaq O'Neal~~ was paid more for his advertising of Nike shoes than all the workers in South Korea received for making them.

We were all horrified. Something should be done. Some insisted we should boycott the goods coming out of these countries. Others looked to the United Nations. Most of the media had a field day blasting the United States for buying these products. The Women's Movement took up the cause in Canada working on several fronts, including going to the United Nations. The cause was noble in inception, but through pressure from many of the countries represented at this august body, it was subverted into imposing big restrictions on the very countries where children were being coddled rather than exploited. For example, children should be free from parents' restrictions on what they read or who they hang out with. How these rights relate to childhood slavery was never explained. It seemed to hinge on the fact that the Developed World must lead the way.

All very well and good you may ask, but how does this translate to the public school system? The Mulroney government instituted a program whereby Elections Canada organized a "child vote" in 250 schools across the country. The main objective of this project was to promote the details of the U.N. Charter of the Rights of a Child (accepted by Canada in 1991) and ask *these immature students* to choose their favorite right among the ones included. It turned out to be a great way to subvert the rights of parents over their children, as well as the rights of teachers over their students.

Another project featured two Columbian teenagers touring the country urging students to assert their rights in spite of objections by parents, and possibly other authority figures. After 25 years of the Canadian Charter of Children's Rights (1982) plus that of the United Nations, is it any wonder that children in public seem to be uncontrolled and verbally abusive to all adults including their parents? More specifically, here we have a terrible example of how schools have been used to advance the agendas of some groups. How is this different from the religious schools of the past? Such are the methods used by many of the extremist Islamic schools of today that train young people to commit to jihad. Hitler's Youth Camps and Stalin's KGB training camps did the same thing. I maintain that schools should beware of noble purposes lest they be subverted to accommodate the agendas of some special interest group. Schools would be well advised to steer clear.

5. <u>Anti-Smoking and Tobacco</u> - I confess that in the beginning I supported efforts against smoking. Most teachers smoked; during breaks the staffroom would be suffused with cigarette smoke, the furniture would reek, and the eyes of non-smokers would smart with irritation. I welcomed the news of groups organizing against smoking. By the 1980's, anti-smoking lessons had become part of Health classes and soon spread to other Humanities subjects, perhaps not as whole lessons, but as examples of unacceptable behavior and habits, as were debates, discussions, and essays on this subject. Sometimes prizes were given out for the best essay on the use of tobacco, with fingers clearly pointing to the side most likely to yield a positive result.

Again going to extremes, the pressure group associated with this movement soon decided that school walls should shelter a ban on smoking by everyone including staff, who soon were found huddling outside the back doors during breaks. The caretakers were luckier often finding spots in furnace rooms or other dark corners. Ironically, despite the fact that children under 18 years old could not purchase tobacco or cigarettes legally, the school front doors often were places where the teenagers hung out to smoke. Harsh penalties imposed on corner stores for selling cigarettes to minors were not extended to the minors themselves for actually consuming this substance. Now whole communities, even cities have become smoke-free zones and those unfortunate souls (usually productive members of society or veterans of wars) who still smoke despite these draconian laws, have become the pariahs of post-modern Canada. Schools have been used extensively in this massive campaign. It strikes me that smoking is an adult area of concern and schools should not be the place to promote this message.

6. Similarly, the <u>Anti-Nuclear Campaign</u> of the 1970's and early 1980's was carried on extensively in the schools. What do seven and eight year olds know about the complicated question of whether Canada should be involved in nuclear research and development? For that matter the same question goes for 16 and 17 year olds. Did that matter to the zealots of the anti-nuclear group? Of course not. Children were led out on marches down city streets, posters were hung on hallway walls and media reports were written congratulating students for taking such positive steps. With the hindsight of twenty years or so, most thinking people will now acknowledge that these efforts were premature at best. Europeans, especially the French, have been building nuclear plants for energy for 30 years and now North Americans are finally considering that perhaps nuclear power should be our energy of choice rather than enriching the dangerous Middle East by purchasing their oil. Perhaps one can say that ideas change with new knowledge and experience. Truly then, should we not acknowledge that schools are not the place to propagandize these controversial ideas on immature and vulnerable minds?

7. <u>Multiculturalism</u> – Sometime in the 1970's Trudeau championed the idea of introducing multiculturalism as a part of the curriculum for schools. Presumbably this idea was based on the policy of tolerance for all people regardless of race, creed, or color of skin. If their customs and values seemed somewhat strange, this should not bother us. We were repeatedly told that we were a country of immigrants and therefore should welcome peoples from all corners of the world. It sounded reasonable at first perfunctory exposure, before the policies came into force. Next we

learned that Canada was, unlike the melting pot of the United States, a mosaic of all cultures because we were not going to insist on assimilation. Rather, each culture, religion, whatever, could retain their language and customs, in fact could actually receive tax dollars to achieve this objective. Moreover, these directives were to be partly funded so that schools could help to promote them. Training the young people in schools would be quickest and best way to change the outmoded, racist ideas promulgated by Judeo-Christian values on which Canada had been built.

Those of us from the older generations felt a bit miffed since we believed fervently that Judeo-Christian values were simultaneous with tolerance, understanding, and equality. Furthermore, no one seemed to question the fact that many thousands of these immigrants coming to Canada were actively seeking what Canada had to offer. How could the Old Ways be so anathema to these new pressure group that change must be instituted forthwith and with government largesse? There is an old saying, "Be careful what you wish for, it may come true." And it has.

That policy put a whole new light on the situation. Some of these policies took the form of professional days for teachers, multicultural Social Studies units of study, multicultural Expositions attended by parents and important guests, English as a Second language classes for all groups "where numbers warranted", even preferential hiring of personnel who best reflected these minority groups. Aha, I thought, I will surely be in demand as an English teacher of many years experience. Not so, I soon learned until and unless I finished a special course in Second Language teaching. Teachers of French were brought in from Quebec and elsewhere without these special qualifications for their teaching, but alas, we teachers of English language and literature did not qualify. If I sound a little bitter, I confess, I was and still am. It seemed those of us who were born and bred in Western Canada and over the age of forty were suddenly the last people to be considered as examples and teachers of newly-minted Canadians. It is weird to be considered a stranger in your own land, and that was how many of us felt.

Many traditional customs now came under scrutiny when looked at from this perspective. The Lord's prayer had been eliminated years before, not a bad idea considering that freedom of conscience was part of Canada's Bill of Rights since 1932. Were the Multicultural Gang content with that? Nada. Next in question came cultural holidays such as Easter and even Christmas. By the end of the 1990's, many schools had abolished Christmas concerts, Christmas gift-giving, even the greeting of "Merry Christmas". At the same time cultural sensitivity demanded that other strange customs, costumes, and languages be given special status. Many things became okay as long as they were considered part of someone's religion, yet old "Canadian" symbols seemed not to fit in these categories. Feeble objections to some of these anomalies were immediately lambasted as "Racist". News items started appearing where people were faced with answering to the Human Rights Commission. Big Brother had arrived in force.

8. But by far the worst policy in all this angst was the question of <u>Aboriginal Education and Special Rights for Aboriginals</u>. In light of modern ideas of equality for peoples from around the world who had come here as immigrants, it seemed utterly illogical to insist that one group should be singled out for Special Rights over and above what was being handed out to various cultural groups willy-nilly. From as early as I can remember, Indian children (as they were then called) could attend any public school of their choice. I based this conclusion on the fact that two of them were my classmates from Grade Two on during the 1940's. In all my teaching teaching years later the same policy has continued. How have they been singled out negatively, I wonder?

In those tender awakening years I became aware that these children also had special schools built for them by different religions. Institutions existed as Special Boarding Schools where Indian children only were fed, clothed, and educated for free in the best tradition of the private schools of England. "Why couldn't we, that is, my ten brothers and sisters, attend those schools?" I innocently asked my mother? Her first answer concluded, "...because they were poor." But we were also poor, as witnessed by the second hand clothes handed done from one to the other and the struggle to feed ourselves every day. The real answer finally emerged; they were Indians and had Special Rights agreed to by the Government. Why were they more special than us? My young mind was comforted by the thought that, as I grew older, I would understand this contradiction to common sense and fairness that our government held as one of our most basic values.

As if this wasn't enough to totally warp a young mind which is being reminded daily of how we are all equal citizens, strong and free, made to draw innumerable pictures of the Canadian flag, sing the national anthem about our country "gloriousness" and beg God to "Bless our King/Queeen", conditions continued to deteriorate over the next 50 odd years.

Indians/ Natives/ Aboriginals were rather pathetic creatures at that time. They did seem to be very poor and people did seem to look upon them as second class citizens. Pity, plus direction from my parents and other fair-minded adults, did instill in most of us children the spine to be friendly and supportive of the Indians we met on almost a daily basis living in an area within easy distance of three Indian Reservations. We understood Indians did not have regular citizenship rights of voting and the right to own private property, nor did they have to pay taxes, unless and until they bought themselves off the Reserve. Certain individuals had done this, and curiously it seemed that these were individuals who were no longer any poorer that the rest of us. As Alice opined, "Curiouser, and curioser!"

Then came the late 1950's where Indians were granted full citizenship rights while still retaining all their Indian Rights, notably they still were exempt from all/most taxes. The Red Indian Power Movement began in earnest spilling across the border from the United States. In fact, they do not recognize the border, but now consider they are special Nations unto themselves, empowered to make their own laws while still not having to pay taxes.

Despite all the funding and recognition of Special Rights, most of the Indian conditions did not improve. Education was soon identified as one of the primary causes of their problems and, at the same time, the avenue by which they could dig themselves out of this condition. Those very same schools that I had envied in my youth were painted with the brush of racism, injustice, cultural genocide, discrimination (meaning prejudice), physical abuse, and horrors, even sexual abuse. As most of you are aware, dear readers, Canada and some churches are faced with billions of dollars of reparations for these supposed abuses, plus enumerable hours of negotiation, litigation and need I say frustration. Lawyers are racking up millions of dollars in legal fees, while curiously, the conditions for the recipients still does not seem to be improving.

Their attitudes, however, certainly have changed. Now one seldom hears about whether these conditions are fair or equal, just that these are "entitlements" from the 300 year old treaties. If that were a good argument, we should all be arguing about what we are owed back to at least the Crusades. Certainly slavery should be a recognized social system since it was well-respected at the same time that the treaties were being written. Obviously, both arguments are ridiculous. Past errors and human inequalities should be eliminated in the cause of Individual Rights.

The original church Mission Schools are now abandoned or turned into Healing Circles, for example. During the 1970's, 1980's and 1990's new schools designed by the New York architect, Cardinal, were being built at great expense on obscure Reserves in Alberta and Saskatchewan, often servicing more adult personnel than students. Special schools within the public school systems in cities proudly boast of Aboriginal Programs (we can no longer call them Indians) complete with re-learning the ancient arts of buffalo hide-tanning and beadwork. Private business are besieged with requests for donations to fund field trips, Awareness Days, Daycare services, Drug and Alcohol Treatment programs, the list goes on. Like the Hydra's [Gorgon's] head it seems, just as one need is met three more appear as if out of nowhere.

Administering these schools tends to be a nightmare for whoever is in charge, which can be difficult to ascertain on its own. Children drift from family to family, school to school, changing surnames at will, ignoring any rules saying you must inform the administration when you decide to leave or enter the school. I took the initiative to list my students by first names in my attempt to keep track of attendance. Teachers of Grade 12 especially, desperately searched for ways to get their students to pass the 50% government exams mandated by Alberta Education. No one had passed a Grade 12 Math 30 or Chemistry 30 class in five years in my school, I was told. Physics 30 was not offered because of lack of interest. Above all this, it was curious for me to note, that the several Indian teachers at the school, all had been educated in those hated Mission Schools. Yet we were constantly reminded how terrible they were. How does that compute?

Add to this dismal picture the fact that no school fees can be charged in Indian Reserve Schools while the same is not true in regular public schools. In fact, it is not uncommon for there to be monetary rewards for good attendance and/or achievement in some Reserve schools. If a student proves worthy to get through high school, s/he can access tutoring, living allowances, daycare, counseling, and other services at no personal cost, together with the continuing entitlement of no tuition or book fees. Naturally, other students resent these special rights and taxpayers groan at the extra burden that inevitably gets heavier every year.

The Fraser Institute has published the following statistics in regard to Indian/Aboriginal Education in February of 2004:

"In the last four school years, British Columbia's Aboriginal students failed more than 40% of the province-wide reading tests that they wrote. On every one of the grade 4 and grade 7 test sittings their failure rate was more than double that of their non-Aboriginal classmates.

The likelihood that Aboriginal children enrolling in grade 8 will successfully complete their studies and receive their diplomas in the usual time is only slightly better than one in five. In contrast the non-Aboriginal success rate is more than three times higher.

Aboriginal students take, on average, less than one of the senior level provincially examinable courses whereas their non-Aboriginal counterparts take nearly three. It these courses that prepare students for a wide variety of post-secondary education programs."

All these horror stories are based on the specious argument that the Indian was here first, or that treaties cannot be broken. It does not seem to matter that those treaties were signed by an Empire long dead, in conditions totally different from what they are now. Even the most far-thinking individual could not have foreseen how Western civilization would evolve given the fundamental revolution in societal organization started by the American experiment. I summarize these totally untried and new ideas as (1) freedom of life choices for citizens, (2) private property as the basis of ownership, (3) capitalism as an economic system adhering to written laws, and (4) democracy as the peaceful method of changing our governments after certain time periods. Many of these novel ideas had never been tried before. The fact that they have produced a society of unprecedented wealth and opportunity should be celebrated not forced to atone for supposed "sins" of the past.

In my early years in school a favorite topic for essays involved describing what life in Canada will be like in 30 or 40 years. No descriptions in my recollection were remotely close to what life is really like now. Doesn't that premise preclude our hysterical response to a present-day problem? We seem to have lost the ability to use our common sense, or to face the facts squarely and admit how wrong-headed has been our approach to this problem. How can past generations be used as an argument for maintaining treaties in their original (or interpreted) form? Further, how can majority vote be used to foist on one group of people the burden of financing another forever and forever "until the sun doesn't shine, or the rivers run uphill"? Is this not he definition of slavery which we proudly proclaim was abolished in the 19th century? Teachers must try to answer these always in a positive light as regards public policy.

The definition of a citizen in my estimation, is one who is born here or comes here legally and willingly accepts our laws and values. Furthermore, she/he has attained the age of majority, and pays taxes to support the system. One hopes that generally, a citizen will contribute in other ways to the country, such as taking up arms to defend it, but this condition is not mandatory, nor should it be. Need I add, however, that Canada made her mark as a respected country in her own right on the backs of men and women in the two World Wars when they did not have that latter choice. These men and women have no special rights, why should anyone else?

As an afterthought, it bugs me that I cannot call myself a Native in the accepted definition of that word. My father's family came here at least two hundred years ago. My mother's family came here in the beginning of the twentieth century at a time when all they were offered was land for ten dollars per quarter section and the freedom to live or starve as part of the conditions of free choice. In Saskatchewan at thirty degrees below zero I am sure they prayed diligently that they had not made a terrible mistake. Today's immigrants are coddled like infants in comparison. Meanwhile, neither I nor millions like me, cannot call ourselves Native. We are hyphenated Canadians, while the Indian reserves this Right, blessed by our government, for themselves. Anyone with me?

Finally, besides all these special entitlements, how else does this policy translate to public schools in other ways? Since the Indian Act is part of our laws, schools are required to promote the official government policy in a myriad of way such as, it means elementary and senior Social Studies courses must include projects and chapters on aboriginal communities, generally focusing on the positive aspects of aboriginal lives before white man came, how the Amerindians helped the European immigrants, and that they gave up their land willingly, not through necessity.

Children are required to write essays on Aboriginal Rights and/or participate in debates. Test items on this topic appear in exams, et cetera. I could go on, but I will be branded a racist if I do. The Truth is no defence, so I will end here. Research the rest yourself, and see if what I have said is based on anything but the objective facts.

9. <u>C.A.L.M., 1985.</u> – stands for Career and Life Management. It was the brainchild of a group of educators who were sure parents were too busy and too clueless to teach their children how to cook breakfast, clean their rooms, manage their money, and cope with the pressures of sexuality. Basically, I suspect, their hidden agenda was to further erode the rights of parents. Hence, out sprang the Career and Life Management Program fully formed from "the forhead of Zeus" so to speak. Curriculum was rather vague, leaving much up to the "interest and special skills" of the instructor. Marks were generally based on attendance and "participation".

My children were in high school at the time; my husband and I were both teachers, and even we were taken by surprise at the rapidity with which it appeared. Our daughter escaped by one year from this compulsory subject and thus was able to take an extra Chemistry course. Our son lost one-half a semester of typing and computers as a result. Next year, in 1988, in Alberta, it became a full course and students have been suffering its inanity and subsequent loss of one worthwhile subject as a result ever since.

I recall being introduced to C.A.L.M. as the subject where students would be given information on and experience with career choices, especially the thousands of new careers in science and technology, and information on post secondary institutions associated with their training. If the school had stuck to this area of concern as an OPTION for those students wanting it, I could support it wholeheartedly. But this was not good enough. C.A.L.M. became a compulsory subject for all high school students regardless of their interests, and teachers were often coerced into teaching it. I wondered why counselors were not the obvious choice as teachers of this subject. It would have got them out of their offices and forced them to teach rather than have comfy little one–on-ones with the student body.

Of course, I realize I am a dinosaur. I believe that a teacher is not worthy of the name unless he/she actually TEACHES more that a group of three at once. Three or less is a TUTOR. Zero students is not a teacher, whatever else they wish to be called.

Teachers did the best they could, given the general nature of the mandate, and the fact that you as a teacher, are required to motivate your students and keep them in class at all costs. Naturally, the subject matter soon came into conflict with rules parents had at home, certainly in the area of sexual behavior, a subject which will "motivate" children of that age if nothing else will. Students were taught to become familiar with "their sexuality" including such experiences as tasting vaginal cream and putting condoms on bananas. Tolerance for different lifestyles became a byword for promoting homosexuality and bisexuality as merely a lifestyle choice, yet when the abstinence movement tried to gain a foothold, they were rebuffed time and again. So much for tolerance.

Suffice to say, despite the fact that students found multiple reasons for staying away and parents felt embattled and undermined, graduates joke about how easy the course was. Another increduality was that some people actually failed it (" he/she didn't come the minimum number of times). Disappointingly, most of the career information consisted of students researching their career of choice by themselves in front of a computer program. Nevertheless, the C.A.L.M. course continues to this day in Alberta and receives no government criticism or re-evaluation that I know of.

In my opinion this program should be abolished as a compulsory subject. Only then will we find out how much true support it has from both parents and students. From all reports that I have heard and experienced it is largely a waste of valuable time, and at worst, a source of severe irritation between school and parents.

10. <u>Sign Your Organ Donor Cards</u> - was another pressure group allowed into the High Schools. This one sends chills down my spine. I guess it is a great and beautiful thing to be so charitable, but to pressure young people to sign their donor cards by health care professionals inside a classroom seems to me we are going over the top. Most of them know that young people, particularly young men, have the most accidental deaths due to dangerous driving and general testosterone, so discussing it becomes a rather morbid subject in that context. I really think parents should be the ones who give their children permission to attend such a session, and that probably they should be there as well. The implications of this practice cannot help but enter into your mind despite trying to keep it out. What if you aren't really dead when they decide to take your organs? Do you really trust your government or your doctor to that extent that they would NEVER make a bad decision?

I think I heard this lecture for the first time in 1988. Eighteen years later, horror stories have seeped out from various corners of the world so my squeamishness has not exactly been for nought. (Access Falun Gong in the Internet) I don't want to say any more on that subject.

Hundreds more Pressure Groups spring up every year. Charitable drives for one or another of various unimpeachable good works, are further examples, another is the arguments for (seldom against) Gun Control or Abolition. I think we should keep them out of the schools as much as possible. They are always emotional issues, are generally accompanied by group hysteria, and rarely have been well thought-out. What is trendy one year is as dead as dishwater five years later. Usually they are judged to be important and factual merely by the numbers of people who will join a parade or demonstration. "Group think" and mob rule has accounted for some of the worst examples of man's inhumanity to mankind, and animal-kind , and environment-kind for that matter. Let's keep it out of the schools. Let parents and community groups shoulder this potentially dangerous burden.

CHAPTER SEVEN – DRESS CODE

"Eat to please yourself, but dress to please others."
Benjamin Franklin, 1706-90

This chapter will be very short since the topic is so specific. However, whether the impact of this subject should also be of little importance needs to be examined. In my opinion, the use of uniforms and/or at least a strict dress code has a significant impact on education..

Children, especially teenagers, have a natural inclination to defy their parents' desires and their cultures' mores. It appears to be part of the hard-wired traits from our evolutionary past. This revolutionary spirit may be the cause of exactly why human progress has occurred, so deserves to be considered, discussed, and researched.

In the past 400 years of more or less free-but-not-mandatory education for the middle to upper classes in England, history has shown that school uniforms were accepted without question. It is only in our new continent of North America, namely Canada and the United States, that the practice of voluntary dress code has become the norm. One can understand this standard being acceptable in the distant rural communities which made up the bulk of our communities up to the mid 1900.s. Families back then generally were extremely poor. It was difficult for parents to provide two sets of clothing for their children, one set for work, and one good set for Sunday Church or special occasions. To expect them to also pay for special uniforms for school was basically a pipe dream. Realistically speaking, many children would have had to sacrifice education *per se* if uniforms had become mandatory.

In addition, textile factories were few and far between, so much so that it would have been extremely difficult to supply such a demand.

Other considerations need to be examined as well. One of the purposes for the use of identifiable uniforms for children included security from invasion by outsiders as well as their use as an advertising medium.. A school uniform made it easier to determine the worth of your school. Reputations for competence were built on the excellence of scholarship provided by that school as witnessed by its graduates' successes and contributions to society in later life. School uniforms, particularly ties for boys, were treasured and proudly displayed by British Isles citizens and ex-patriots.

Transplanted to North America, these ideas have survived in the Ivy League Colleges and Universities to this day. However, the use of uniforms or particular school dress for public elementary through high schools has largely disappeared in our dedication to freedom of choice. Nobody seems to remember that such freedoms applied only to adult citizens. However, as the years have passed and conditions have changed, use of school uniforms continues to come up again and again.

In the outback country of pioneer days, security was rarely a problem, as it now is. Invasion by strangers from the outside community was almost unheard of in small communities where everyone knew everyone else. Furthermore, schools were few and far between, so the question of identifying children by the school which they attended was an unnecessary luxury. Such is not the case today. Most of us live in major cities where security has become an increasing problem. We are assailed almost weekly by reports of school lock-downs or violence in or one the school grounds, notwithstanding that many of these incidents are not reported openly. Intruders must be identified. Visitors to the schools are admonished to check in with the administration office by prominent signs posted near the entrances. As we all know, the visitors who obey these signs are the parents and other honorable people. As a parent and now volunteer this makes me feel somewhat unwelcome, while the sign does not affect anyone who wishes to do harm. A person of less that stellar reputation, or one intending to do harm will purposely ignore these signs.

One of the solutions that I actually recommended as far back as 1992 was to install surveillance cameras in these entrances. Now cameras in school entrances are standard in many if not most schools. However, cameras are only as good as their continual surveillance which has its limitations not the least of which are the increased costs.

The latest example of a school invasion as of this writing involved a hostage-taking of six young girls and the tragic murder of one of them. It occurred in Dawson, Colorado, on September 13, 2006. The perpetrator was described as a middle-aged man, head covered in a "hoodie", who was able to pass himself off as one of the students for enough time to carry out his despicable intent. Had school uniforms been the code in this school it is unlikely that this event could have occurred so easily.

I, and most classroom teachers, have had similar experiences with "hoodies". They fit over the arms, half the body, and completely over the head. Conveniently equipped with several pockets they are very useful for carrying small objects. When pulled close it is very difficult to tell whether the person is a boy or a girl, older or younger. They are cheap to buy and a perfectly acceptable kind of all-weather jacket. The "hoodie" has become the apparel of choice for petty thieves and break-in artists specifically because of these precise features. They have also become a fashion statement for certain groups of school children. It was not uncommon to have one-quarter of a class dressed in one of these, particularly in remedial classes.

Institution of school uniforms, or at least strict enforcement of school dress codes would do much to alleviate some of these security and propriety problems for the school as a whole as well as for the classroom teachers. I have dealt with girls in school wearing clothes fit for prostitutes only - string shoulder straps and necklines cut down to cleavage, bare midriffs clearly exposing hip bones, sometimes even rear end cleavage, and clothes so tight one wonders how they can breathe. Add to these distracting dress packages, the Gothic Look is "in" featuring black nail polish and black lipstick not to mention the steel or silver studs in parts of the body not fit to mention. Boys have differing, but equally distracting apparel. Sometimes they have worn such tight jeans as to be fearful they would damage their manhood, then conversely pants so loose and baggy that they were forced to walk from the knees downward. And, in so many cases, the ubiquitous ball cap, either pulled low over the eyes or turned backward, sometimes even sideways.

However much teenagers declare that their choice of clothing styles is not necessarily a mark of gang associations, experience has proven, beyond a doubt, that 90% of the time adults are correct in concluding that these students are not ready to learn, to say the least. It is a way of thumbing their nose at the authority figure, saying in essence, "Just try to teach me. I'm going to make it as difficult as possible for you."

Hair and dress styles have been used as outward signs of belief in or evidence of religious conviction, cultural mores, and societal classes since the dawn of history. It is part of what makes us human. Women spend hours in angst wondering what to wear to a certain event so as not to be underdressed or overdressed, often telephoning friends to ask, "What are you wearing?" Men usually display themselves to their wives who seem to have a better sense of style, at least once men have passed the young manhood stage. It is time we faced the facts of human nature and instituted uniforms for school children so we can forget this great time and money waster, as well as save our teachers from hours of emotional turmoil, and concentrate, instead, on students' education.

In most schools of my experience, dress codes were discussed from time to time, but came to little of substance. During staff meeting the question of whether to allow the wearing of ball caps or hoods became a frequent topic. The resulting conclusion was generally that schools would be taking on too much of a risk. It seems that fear of a lawsuit based on Canada's Charter of Rights and Freedoms trumped all considerations, even school safety. Later, signing onto the United Nations Convention on the Rights of the Child in 1991 further exacerbated the situation. In its zeal to protect children from exploitation and abuse, this charter requires signatory states to

> ".... exercise their parental responsibilities. The Convention also acknowledges that children have the right to express their opinions and to have those opinions heard and acted upon when appropriate …. and requires that their lives not be subject to excessive interference.'

> "The Convention also obliges signatory states to provide separate legal representation for a child in any judicial dispute concerning their care." (Wikipedia. Convention on the Rights of the Child. May, 2007)

In other words the Child was accorded exceptional rights and supplanted the State as the main arbiter over the parents in regards to their own children. This action has resulted in great reluctance by school authorities to put limits on children's preferences in regard to dress. Inevitably, teachers' meetings would usually end with the decision to distribute a newsletter to parents, or hold a public meeting. If even one parent objected the matter was dropped.

Then next step meant memorandums would be distributed about what might be considered acceptable dress, but *IT WAS UP TO THE CLASSROOM TEACHER TO ENFORCE WHATEVER DRESS CODE THEY WISHED* based on these guidelines. If you couple this directive with the Top Down model of school management, you can appreciate what an impossible situation this became for the teacher. If you tried to implement a rule of no ball caps in your room, you became the favorite target for attacks. "But Mr. Smith, or Ms. Johnson lets us wear them, " chant the choruses. If you are lucky, you find yourself spending a big part of any period dealing with enforcement. With persistence, and if you have established tenure and a good reputation in the school, you may succeed. More normally, one or more of the students would complain to the principal, their parents, or the counselor about this huge intrusion into their freedom of choice, and you would be forced to defend your stance. You as the teacher have become the awful face of exception to the unwritten rules. In my experience, whenever the specter of litigation appeared around the corner, the authority figures faded into the safe corners.

It is just not worth it. This kind of a directive must come from the highest authority, at least in the particular school for it to become a standard rule. Ideally, there should be a set of dress standards for all the public schools in one jurisdiction. Students are well aware of the tactic of divide and conquer, and of playing one side against another, even if they can't articulate this timeworn principle. By their very nature, children react emotionally to attempts to curtail their preferences. It is silly of us adults to allow them to make decisions on such serious subjects.

Let us examine some of the research.

Attempts to encourage school uniforms became a major impetus of the American Presidency during the mid 1990's. Several studies were conducted. The largest of these and the one most quoted on use of school uniforms was carried out through the auspices of the United States Federal government in 1993-95. Statistical data was collected by the Long Beach Unified School District for Grades 4 through 9 in 56 elementary and 14 middle schools. Despite the difficulty of carrying out a truly scientific study on this question, several positive influences became evident. There were dramatic reductions in assaults, vandalism, theft, and drug use. Robbery decreased by 65%. Overall crime rate decreased by 91%. Suspensions decreased 36% in middle school and 28% in elementary school. Attendance reached an all-time high. Five years following completion of the study, suspensions were down by 90%. (Google Internet research. Family Education.com. *School Uniforms: Pros and Cons.* July, 2007)

Detractors were quick to point out that there was no absolute proof that these results were directly correlated to school uniforms. Most of the surveys regarding its effectiveness proved inconclusive, they pointed out because of the difficulty of testing just this element in a non-scientific laboratory like a school. Moreover, an opt-out policy had to be included which possibly skewed the results. K. Seamon and J. Schultink from Michigan State University reported in 2006. "..While the rising poularity is undisputed, uniforms' relative effectiveness remains unclear primarily due to lack of research. Research is often difficult to conduct because the implementation of school uniforms accompanies changes in personnel, curriculum, and other policies. It also may be difficult to find a school system undergoing the change. .." (Seamon & Schultink, Michigan State University, 2006)

Data on the *student perceptions* of whether they liked school uniforms or not were generally negative. Personally, I hold little interest in these type of "feel-good" questions. The factual evidence has much greater impact.

Other objections to implementation of school uniforms range from the costs involved to the message we are sending to our young people. The cost argument is an obvious distraction.

A study in 1996 determined that, for students up to high school level, uniforms cost approximately $70.00 to $90.00 , while typical back to school ordinary dress expenditures cost $375.00. (Costs expressed in U.S. dollars.) (Stanley, 1996)

School uniforms are much cheaper than most other clothing because they can be mass produced. As for the children's free choice argument, the same people who advocate that you should allow young students to decide what they want to study today, have the following argument: "Children should be allowed and encouraged to express their individuality in school as well as the larger society. Grunge, hip-hop, gothic, J. Crew, et cetera ... They're all styles of dressing – each proclaiming its own codes and values. Forbidding adolescents to express themselves through clothing and hairstyles prevents a healthy transition to independence and freedom from their parents and other adults." (Google Internet on School Uniforms. FamilyEducation.com, July, 2007).

This argument is highly specious if not egregious. Children do not have to suffer personally for any mistakes that they make. Besides which they are very immature and inexperienced and often make decisions based on immediate gratification much to their dismay later. As adults and parents it is up to us to decide what is best for them until they go out on their own. We must act as responsible adults in this area of concern. Asking the children what they want is okay in a family setting, but it remains for the adults to make the final decision because whether you do so or not, you, as their guardian, will have to suffer the consequences when they make foolish, dangerous, or deadly decisions. What is to stop children from dressing in large flowing robes, capable of concealing an automatic gun, not to mention crib notes for cheating? This dress could even be demanded as part of their religious beliefs. How does the teacher deal with that? How safe is that?

Is it not curious that many businesses have dress codes, particularly the ones dealing with the public. If one enters most large grocery chains all the clerks have similar uniforms, and I have it from a worker that these are mandated by the administration, nationwide. Most of the large department stores have special smocks, at least, for their clerks. It makes it easier to know who to ask for help. I remember the time when hospitals had strict uniforms for different staff levels. How nice it was to know the difference between nurses, aides, doctors, orderlies, et cetera. When our son was in the hospital in 1998 it was very confusing not to know whom to ask for various services. Banks used to have strict dress codes, but now you occasionally see some of the young tellers with scanty costumes and steel rings in eyebrows, noses, even tongues. I don't like it and on one occasion asked to have another teller deal with me on something as serious as money. Funny how these new regulations on personal choice for dress seems to coincide very handily with the appearance of our vaunted Human Rights Commissions which are now championing opposition to our freedom of speech. Perhaps some relaxation of the tight collars and heavy suit jackets were in order, but as usual they have "just gone nuts". (refer again to Ted Byfield in *Alberta Report*) The relationship to school dress codes is obvious. If work conditions often require specifications on dress, why not for our children?

Now let's look at school uniforms from the perspective of the parents for a minute. Thousands if not millions of parents would find their lives simplified immensely by this simple solution. No longer would they find themselves beseiged by hours of nagging from children determined to have the designer label so necessary to maintain a proper posture in school. They would also save money, maybe enough for a decent family vacation. Less clothing would be scattered on the bedroom floor by children dressing and undressing to get just the right thing to wear. Be honest, friends, our modern affluent society means we have multiple choices in clothing, but still there is a question of just which is the correct pair of jeans to wear. I once complemented a niece of mine on her excellent choice of jeans, asking what brand they were. She casually remarked that she had 16 pairs so it appeared different occasions called for different labels. It was a new one on me.

Likewise, our children are conditioned to want to be in with the crowd. Whether we like it or not, they are adhering to a dress code, worrying excessively over which outfit to chose that day instead of concerning themselves with academia. The research did show in general that although students, especially high school students, did object to uniforms, they generally admitted they got used to them and liked them after awhile, and they did seem to make the school safer. (Anthony Poet, principal of Puebla Del Sol Middle School, Arizona, 2006) Let us take a huge burden off their shoulders and ours, and institute school uniforms as quickly as possible.

In conclusion, I wish to add that I acknowledge my son-in-law (whose name I will omit for personal reasons) for his input on this serious subject. He wrote his Masters thesis on just this topic and passed on to me much of the information he gleaned as a result. His conclusion was much the same as mine, as well it was partly based on personal experience in a school system where school uniforms were a normal part of school life. No one, neither parents nor children, were anxious to return to the "old" system of personal dress choice for school.

CHAPTER EIGHT – BACK TO BASICS

"All art, all education, can be merely a supplement to nature."
Aristotle, (384-322 B.C,)

What a phrase -- Back to Basics! This argument has been raging for decades, ever since the introduction of John Dewey's conclusion that English was so far from a phonetic language that teaching phonics merely confused small children. Almost one hundred years later, by far the largest segment of Educators are still on the side of "progressive" methods for teaching English. This segment includes the bulk of the Education Establishment including Leaders of Teachers' Colleges, the Heads of Big Teachers' Unions, and the bureaucracies of the Departments of Education while parents, business, and the barely literate graduates wonder why the huge amounts spent on schooling does not seem to be achieving the desired results. Governments are admonished almost daily with the need for more dollars for education while taxpayers cringe at the thought.

John Dewey (1859-1952) provided the main impetus for overturning phonics in teaching reading, starting in the early 1900's. His credentials seem impeccable. He received a B.A. from University of Vermont in 1879 and a Ph.D from John Hopkins University in 1884. He then went on to teach at the University of Michigan, the University of Minnesota, the University of Chicago, and Columbia University, retiring in 1931. His interest and research into education piqued while he was teaching at the University of Chicago where he established the famous Dewey School in 1896. This institution gave him the opportunity to try out some of his new theories. He also wrote nine books as well as lectured and toured educational systems in China, Japan, Mexico, Turkey, and the Soviet Union. For some unknown reason his research did not include Great Britain where English had been successfully taught to thousands of children for 400 years, usually commencing at five years old. Many of his ideas were revolutionary and radical, following in the footsteps of William James, a contemporary philosopher from Harvard University.

Nothing is as important in primary education as learning how to read, write, and do simple mathematics. These were called the three R's -- Reading, 'Riting, and 'Rithmetic. To learn this simple rule one had to spell and write the words phonetically rather than correctly, and slur over the pronunciation and and spelling of Arithmetic, but everyone past Grade Three has heard the phrase. Few know that this learning was true in Western Canada prior to 1945, but has largely faded from the school scene since. Progressive ideas of education has been the basis on which public schools have been conducted for the last three quarters of a century often unacknowledged and sometimes unknown to the majority of the population who are directly paying for it. In many ways this lack of recognition has been used as a convenient scapegoat for any of the failures or difficulties of the Education Establishment.

In one aspect, Dewey was correct. Many English words are not pronounced phonetically, and, ironically, these words are some of the most common in the English language. Therefore, a young child encountering reading for the first time is confronted with exceptions to the rule at every turn.. However, since many of these words are the most common ones, it doesn't take long before the child recognizes them on sight with little or no difficulty. I have a list of the 100 most common English words which makes up about one-half of all the words we read and write. 98% of children should find little difficulty in learning to read that many words on sight, certainly within two years. Compare memorizing 100 words with the expectations for Chinese students, who, apparently, have the daunting task of learning 33,000 different symbols by the fifth grade.

Dewey and his disciples came to a different conclusion, however. They maintained that teaching English by "sounding out" words merely confused youngsters rather than helping them. They went to great pains to show that efficient readers take in whole words at once, rather than letter by letter. They communicated this "fact" in thousands of papers and articles written for professionals.

Dewey's research into the study of linguistics was influenced greatly by James M. Cattrell, an American psychologist from the late 1800's. Cattrell,s experiment was to briefly expose subjects to whole words, then individual letters, then ask them what they saw. (*Scientific American*, March, 2002) Cattrell found that his subjects were much better able to remember words than letters. This led him to conclude that people read by taking in whole words at once, not letter by letter. Since phonics is based on sounding out letters and letter combinations, he concluded, as did Dewey, that reading was based on seeing words as a whole. He reasoned that teaching students letter by letter would make for slow and hesitating readers, not a great outcome as students grew older. Together with several other educators Dewey concluded that the English language would be better taught by using scrutiny and memorization rather than phonics to decipher the written word. Educators are still straining to teach English in the American and Canadian public schools based primarily on this premise.

Had Dewey and his colleagues kept open minds on this subject, they may have discovered the flaw. The great flaw in this conclusion was not exposed for many years, in fact we are still arguing about it as I write. More recent research has revealed that adults read whole words at once having seen these words thousands if not millions of times, and therefore automatically take in the whole word. However, when first encountering a new, unknown word (as children must do when learning to read), we look for clues in the single letters or small combinations of letters for both pronunciation and meaning. After we "sound it out" the word often becomes recognizable from our verbal association. Children especially, "light up" as they realize, "I know that word!" (*Scientific American,* March, 2002)

I used this method at home with both my children (to a lesser extent) and with my six-year old granddaughter (to a greater extent, along with her parents' help and cooperation.). Both experiments were very successful and gratifying when the child responded in just this fashion. "I know that word!" Interestingly enough, my granddaughter, Jade, was currently enrolled in a French language immersion program where she had all her regular instruction in French. Therefore, success in reading English was definitely not a result of the exposure she received in school. She learned to read English by the phonics method of decoding letters and letter combinations. By the end of Grade One she was reading books normally used by Grade 3 and 4 students. Now, in Grade Two she reads adult signs on billboards, street signs, advertisements, basically everything. She doesn't understand all that she reads, but she can read it with little difficulty. Naturally, I realize this was largely an uncontrolled experiment, but it was heartwarming to see how easily she learned.

Joe Freedman, a physician from Red Deer, Alberta, did extensive research in the early 1990's comparing results of international results in the core subjects. He published his findings in 1993 in a video and a small booklet entitled <u>Failing Grades.</u> One of his conclusions reads as such "Apart from a number of influential and defensive educational leaders, most knowledgeable Canadians agree that the quality of the K-12 system of education is seriously wanting." (page 6) and later he quotes from *A Lot to Learn: Education and Training in Canada* "If these figures do not improve, our school system will produce well over one million new functional illiterates over the next 10 years." He was right. Statistics

Canada reported in 2005 that "..About two in five adults aged 16 to 65 score below desired threshold (of literacy)". Also from the same report came this statement "Little change in literacy proficiency between 1994 and 2003." That translates into far more than one million, rather approximately seven million Canadian adults appear to have great difficulty in coping with reading as a necessary part of modern life.

Another of the major planks of Dewey's platform was that school should be a place of pleasure, where children loved to come. Lessons must be designed to be fun, not for sitting and listening quietly, then practicing by doing dull drills or memorizing by rote. This idea of fun as opposed to bookwork appealed to the vast majority of people. Who in his right mind would prefer to painfully memorize The Periodic Table, for example, than to sit and watch a video of adorable cartoon characters working in a mad scientist's lab, starring Brad Pitt against that giant enemy Time? Moreover, no one needs to memorize when we can always go to the Internet. The problem appeared later that, although the students were greatly entertained, they retained very little of what they had seen a few hours later. Another problem with entertainment appears to be that in order to be entertainment it must be new and different almost every time, a difficulty that most teachers find insurmountable from the perspectives of time, budget and personal knowledge, not to mention ability. Finally, although computers have become smaller and more portable it is still not as easy to access as that ten pound rounded bulk each one of us has on the top of his shoulders.

Dewey also premised his ideas on democracy, reasoning that education was far too autocratic and therefore not designed for a democracy like the United States. This was an age of progress where new things were being tried every day. Thus was born an entirely new method of teaching English. Children were exposed to a limited number of written words, 350 to be exact in Grade One, gradually increasing the number of words so that by Grade Three they had a reading vocabulary of 1250 words. When one considers that an average child of six years has a speaking vocabulary of 10,000 words on average, it means the stories they could read were extremely contrived. I recall that both as a student and later as a teacher, students were restrained from reading ahead in the book by having a rubber band encircled around the later pages. Don't laugh. This rubber band was an official policy of the School Board in my first school. Later, the curriculum would include some spelling rules, prefixes, suffixes, root words incidentally, as the child needed them. This method became known as the Look-Say Method (also known as the Whole Word or Sight Reading method) and was inculcated in the Dick and Jane series of readers.

Dewey's ideas caught on swiftly and soon there were many scholars and teachers advocating his ideas. Beginning about 1930, most of the United States adopted his ideas on public education. These new, progressive teaching and learning method have been largely in place in all public schools, meaning tax funded , "free" schools for the last sixty to seventy years throughout United States and Canada since then. I believe these same methods were tried briefly in the United Kingdom, but were abandoned shortly afterward. I entered public school in 1946, and happily opened a brand new *Look and See* reader. My oldest sister, Elaine, had taught me how to read by flash cards before I went to school so I don't remember any difficulty in learning to read myself. But I do remember being very frustrated by the lack of more reading material. When I started teaching in 1959 I was using the same series which lasted for about another ten years. Then the Dick and Jane series was abandoned partly because changing textbooks became *de riguer* in the scheme of things. Teachers breathed a sigh of relief because reading Dick and Jane was terribly boring for them as well.

Meanwhile, many shortcomings and weaknesses in this method of teaching reading had become evident years before. Rudolph Flesch wrote *Why Johnny Can't Read* in 1957. He had become a tutor for a young boy named Johnny. This is one of the first few paragraphs.

"Since I started to work with Johnny, I have looked into this whole reading business. I worked my way through a mountain of books and articles on the subject. I talked to dozens of people, and spent many hours in classrooms, watching what was going on.

"What I found was absolutely fantastic. The teaching of reading -- all over the United States, in all schools, in all textbooks -- is totally wrong and flies in the face of all logic and common sense. Johnny couldn't read until half a year ago for the simple reason that nobody ever showed him how. Johnny's only problem was that he was unfortunately exposed to an ordinary American school.

" You know that I was born and raised in Austria. Do you know that there are no remedial reading cases in Austrian schools? Do you know that there are no remedial reading cases in Germany, in France, in Italy, in Norway, in Spain --- practically anywhere in the world except in the United States? Do you know that there was no such thing as remedial reading in this country either until about thirty years ago? Do you know that the teaching of reading never was a problem until the United States switched to the present method around about 1925? " (Flesch, Rudolf, *Why Johnny Can't Read*, 1957)

You can forgive Flesch for not including Canada because few people knew much about what was going on in Canada, certainly not what was going on in our public schools in Western Canada. It is a strange phenomenon that so much of what the States does is not appreciated in Canada, except for Education. We have followed blindly in their steps, never bothering, it seems, to question whether we were doing the right thing or not. What a wasted opportunity we had! Let them go ahead and experiment with new, untested ideas in education, then we could evaluate and adopt or not as results became known. Nay, not so. "What California did must be good for Canadian schools" seemed to be the favorite motto.

Interestingly enough, remedial classes were not something schools adopted until the 1970's to the best of my knowledge. Since then they have proliferated, with little success in my estimation. In fact, many writers and observers of education have cautioned parents against enrolling their child in remedial classes. Once in, it seems he or she is forever scarred, and seldom helped. I have been in several of these remedial classes 'trying to teach" as one positive Teachers' project pointed out. (ATA Magazine, circa 1993) I could see little difference from an ordinary classroom, except for fewer students (usually not more than 10) consisting of individual programs for each student The students worked on worksheets for the most part as their counterparts were doing in the regular classes, interrupted every few minutes by the need to sharpen a pencil, go to the bathroom, ask the kid in front or back for something, and generally waste time. Scuffles broke out every so often which was mainly my job to try to stop it without causing a disruption for the school. Because they were all in different places it was generally impossible to appeal to the whole class. Whenever I would try to engage the whole class I was met with strong objections. The students, generally, seemed to enjoy not making any progress. I have to agree with the general impression from outside, "Do whatever you must, to keep your hyperactive underachiever from getting into one of the remedial classes." Go visit one if you doubt what I say.

I maintain that much of the reason for students needing remediation in reading English is because they have been taught incorrectly at the beginning. Those who doubt my words, please think back to when you were a child. Recall how vivid those early memories are where memories are etched deeply into the mind of a child. Psychologists call this the fact that children have a "tabula rasa" or blank memory. Things a person learns for the first time remain much longer and more clearly than those attained later in life. This fact becomes more and more clear as one gets into the "golden years". Trying to correct a memory later takes more than double the effort. So I urge parents to be extra careful about the methods used for teaching your children the first basics of education. If your school/teacher is not convinced of phonics, you would be well advised to send her/him to one of the excellent academies listed in Chapter Five.

Hilda Neatby's book had pre-empted Flesch by several years. She, too, expressed grave concern about many of the practices in the public schools, but not specifically about teaching reading. I have encountered and read many other articles and books on this subject, among them:

1. Dan Smoot in the Dan Smoot Report, April, 1970. He made a strong case for the old McGuffy readers as better than the present readers being then used. Costs of education were discussed as well. (Incidentally, a few of the McGuffy Readers were still on the shelf in my Grade One school. I remember reading them with great pleasure after being rubber-banded from continuing with *Look and See*
2. The Phyllis Schlafly Report, September, 1985 – "*Phonics – The Key to Reading*".
3. Failing Grades by Dr. Joe Freedman ,1993.
4. "Group wants back-to-basics school" in Calgary Herald, January, 1996.
5. "How should reading be taught" by Raynor, Foorman, Perfetti, Pesetsky and Seidenberg in Scientific American, March, 2002.
6. Project 2006 by the Association for the Advancement of Science in Skeptic Magazine, #3 issue, 2006. "American students will continue to lag behind many of their European and Asian peers."

Besides these books and articles, some very good studies have been done. In 1987, the Southam chain of newspapers conducted an exhaustive series of tests for literacy in both the U.S. and Canada concluding that approximately 25% of citizens in these countries were functionally illiterate, most having attended many years in the public schools. Functionally illiterate means that these people have great difficulty in reading literature related to such things as newspapers, medical instructions on prescriptions, technical manuals, even road signs. At that time I was sure the Education Establishment would pay attention and seek to reverse the decisions on teaching phonics. Sadly, it didn't happen.

Change has occurred, make no mistake about it. In fact, change is a way of life in the schools. So many new courses, new texts, new methodologies, new diagnoses of learning disabilities, et cetera are introduced every year that many teachers are hard-pressed to cope. But will they as a group accept that teaching reading should be done the phonics way? No such luck. The closest the authorities will come to acknowledging the problem is to conclude, with reservations that "..phonics is <u>one</u> of several acceptable methods of teaching reading, but is certainly not the only method. Different children need different approaches." (<u>ATA Magazine</u>, various articles)

Many new programs have been created to deal with teaching English using phonics. These programs have largely made this subject more interesting than just relying on word drills and diacritical marks so prevalent in the original texts. One such program is called "Open Court". I am not familiar with the details of this program, but it has earned wide acclaim by teachers and schools seriously interested in teaching their young charges to read early and well. Many new programs have been created to deal with teaching English using phonics. You can find them on the shelves of many stores including Staples, The Teachers' Store, and Costco on occasion. Unfortunately, the Education Establishment has not responded by offering a comprehensive program of phonics covering all the basic aspects of reading English. So much the pity.

Governments have also lowered expectations in the more senior English language learning program by eliminating mandatory Supplementary Reading. For example, years ago the study of English took up a much larger amount of school time. I am not talking only about primary grades where language learning took up most of the school hours. In upper grades, English was composed of Literature and Composition. Moreover, scholars were expected to read at least one supplementary book per month, or ten per year. These supplementary books included proportions for fiction, non-fiction, biographies, and drama. The despised Book Reviews were usually a way of proving that you had accomplished this outside reading. Despised or not, the Supplementary Reading program forced students to read more than just the regular course material and helped to enlarge one's vocabulary and knowledge. Maybe it even encouraged parents to read to or with their children during those long winter months. It was one method whereby parents could help out the academic process in a more enjoyable way. I vividly remember my mother reading to us *The Egg and I* while we giggled incessantly over the amusing anecdotes of a struggling pioneer family.

From my own experience I remember the extreme trepidation, verging on panic I felt when called upon to speak in public, another forgotten aspect of the long dead Oral component of Language Arts. Starting in Grade 7 we were required to make at least one or two formal oral presentations every year. Moreover, we all competed in a province-wide project called the Saskatchewan Bryant Oratory. How I dreaded those days! But, surprisingly, the anticipation seemed to be worse than the actual experience. Familiarity fostered calmness in front of my peers. Later, during my first year of College, I recall being so nervous in front of complete strangers that I completely lost my voice during the first presentation. How embarrassing! And how silly to be so limited in public, I thought to myself. So I made a solemn promise to overcome this insane fear and to force myself to speak in public as often as the opportunity presented itself.

It is a promise I have kept. In retrospect I can say that there seems no shortcut to gaining confidence in public speaking than by actually doing it. And what better place to practise public speaking than in the relatively safe atmosphere of a classroom? In the REALLY OLD DAYS students were required to stand when they answered a question during class, but that practice went out with <u>Dick and Jane.</u> The new, progressives directives forbid any teacher in Western Canada from forcing a child to speak or read aloud in class, thereby diminishing his/her language ability. Is it any wonder most conversations among young people consist of hundreds of "like's" "whatever's" and other street slang? Moreover, the original English High School program of separating Literature and Composition has been combined into English, meaning that students today take one half the amount of English classes that graduates pre-1970 studied. Moreover, individual teachers are given wide latitude in what literary selections are taught in class. The result has been that some students take <u>Macbeth</u> or <u>Hamlet</u> twice or three times in three different grades, perhaps because they have moved to a different school, rather than being exposed to at least three Shakespearean plays. Consequently, graduates seldom have a common mental library of English literature to call upon for general knowledge and conversation.

Oral speaking used to be part of the English program. It no longer is mandatory. In fact, it is considered insensitive for a teacher to insist that a student answer or read orally, and definitely not be compelled to make an in-class speech. How then does a teacher find out the level of reading competence of a student? No definitive answer there I found out to my own peril. When I insisted that one of my Grade Eleven students read aloud in class precisely to find out his competence in reading, he complained to the Administration who reprimanded *ME*. Further research yielded the information that this particular student had not passed a major test since his early schooling, having moved numerous times sometimes because of his parents, sometimes by his own request. I suspected that these moves were partly to cover up his lack of literacy. Revealing this information to the Administration did not change the fact that I must desist in this kind of teacher instruction. This incident happened after a considerable absence from teaching on my part, so I was rudely brought up-to-date on the new "expectations" for public education.

Generally, the system has been adjusted to meet the needs of non-academic students. It sounded logical to me since there are many students (at least one-half of the high school population) who merely want to get the Grade 12 Diploma and go out to work or get on with their lives. However, many of these adjustments appeared to be repetitions of what they had taken earlier or watered down to such an extent it was embarrassing to call it a senior class. In addition to the illogical method of teaching reading was added the crazy methods for teaching mathematics, from extremely difficult to barely elementary. Students were first completely confused by the New Math, then bemused by the new program containing little but problem solving. Couple this confusion with the Spiral Curriculum and you have a situation where students often encounter the same concepts year after year without having to master them.

So we can stop wondering how it happens that a student can reach senior grades without learning the basics. If one considers the sum total of poor approach to basic language and mathematics coupled with a "No Failure" policy, a recurring curriculum, and a focus on making students feel good about themselves despite performance, maybe we as the public have to revisit our expectations of what public education means. Or conversely, look for an entirely new model.

I propose the latter. More and more educators interested in no nonsense education believe a return to the method of teaching reading by using sound-letter associations, commonly called phonics, plus a mastery expectation for all the "Basics" of elementary education would help elevate our standardized scores across Canada. As a taxpayer, a concerned grandparent, and a former teacher, I sincerely hope so.

CHAPTER NINE – DEMOCRATIZING DISCIPLINES

"Education commences at the mother's knee, and every word spoken within the hearsay of little children tends towards the formation of character."

Hosea Ballou, from *Aphorisms* by Auden &Kronenberger

Sometime before and during World War II, and perhaps as partly a result of this horrendous happening, education underwent a huge change in terms of scholarly disciplines. These changes were implemented based on the postulate that there is a great deal of carry-over between subjects. Keeping them separate meant people's minds remained fragmented causing misinformation and suspicion among the various professions. Taking this mindset to its extremes, it could be argued that this mental fragmentation could have been partly the cause of various wars. We need more co-operation and understanding among peoples rather than competition. How these two ideas can be linked to education requires a great leap of faith in my estimation. However, educators seemed to accept this premise since they concluded that schools should forego keeping academic disciplines separate and distinct. Instead, the curriculum should seek to show the relationships between disciplines and how they interrelate. Overall, it seemed like a noble objective; in retrospect this premise has had serious negative results on education.

Within 30 years, integrating academic subjects has evolved into a blurring of lines among subjects and the elimination of several. In my years of substituting where I went from one classroom to another it sometimes became difficult to tell what was the actual subject under discussion since many different classes seemed to be focused on primarily the same general theme.

First subject on the chopping block was Geography, and then History. These subjects became the ubiquitous Social Studies. I personally experienced this transition by being in the first grade, 1946, when History and Geography disappeared in Saskatchewan and we were subjected (if you'll pardon the pun) to this new subject. Proudly we opened our new textbooks feeling very special because new textbooks were extremely rare in those small country schools.

Social Studies can be almost anything to do with the study of peoples' history, travels relationships, governments, patriotism, or struggles to understand life in all its vicissitudes. In effect, it can be everything and anything you want it to become. What a perfect vehicle for propaganda and brain washing! And, dear reader, that is precisely what has happened in many classes over the last six plus decades. The most generous conclusion I can attribute to this general trend is to conclude that perhaps this propaganda was not deliberate.

At first, much of the course remained very similar to the old history course for the upper grades and civics for the younger ones. We happily colored Canadian flags, sang O Canada, and learned about England's Royal Family, which transitioned into the story of the British Commonwealth, followed by Canada's development as a nation. High School years covered the gamut from Ancient and Medieval History through Greek and Roman civilizations into the incessant wars scourging the European continent. Our knowledge of geography was taught incidentally as we studied a country or countries. Occasionally we were reminded that mountains, rivers, seas and other natural topography had an effect on many of these struggles. We missed out on important knowledge of how distances, climate, and location can determine much of what happens to a group of people. Even more important, many graduates from public schools know so little about location that they are hard-pressed to tell you where Russia or China is on a map.

On the whole, the history of mankind history was presented as a story of Human Progress. I do not recall any real debate among educators about another perspective. To support this theme, teachers could pick and choose among various periodicals, newspapers, magazines, and occasionally textbooks to support this theme. The problem of copyright was overcome by government decree declaring that as long as it was for education purposes lifting items piecemeal from various sources was okay, without the necessity of acknowledging the source.

The Human Progress theme meant all major happenings in the world were positive, conditions were continuing to get better and better as long as we had majority opinion to back it up. From my perspective of 60+ years I question whether we have fundamentally misdirected our young people. A better theme would be "Constant Vigilance". How else can one explain the Dark Ages after the much more civilized and enlightened times of Greek, Roman, or, Babylonian civilizations, not to mention civilizing accomplishments that had occurred in more remote corners of the world which archeologists are continuing to uncover? How has it happened that Africa is now sliding into an unprecedented era of disease, hunger, terror, and genocide after decades, perhaps even a century of happier times? What's that I hear? How can I defend colonialism, you ask? Was that time not also the era of colonial expansionism? European countries had carved up this unfortunate continent and added these territories to their empires. Anything would be better than that. Really? I wonder what the people of Nigeria sould say? (2 million killed) or Rwanda? (1,020,000 murdered) or Uganda? (900,000 eliminated) and now Zaire, formerly Belgian Congo? (14,000 and counting) who knows what is happening in Zimbabwe. A recent article in the *Calgary Herald* stated, "Life in Zimbabwe is murder these days." (September 26, 2007) Even Kenya, one of the most advanced African nation, is in the midst of a civil war. Maybe we should ask those victims of genocide. Oh, I forgot. They are all dead. (All statistics relate to the 1900's, from *National Geographic,* January, 2006.)

I have grave concerns about that theme as our general approach to Social Studies. The Twentieth century has seen at least 9 million people being killed, tortured, and starved by their own petty dictators in Africa, while the United Nations peacekeepers pretend to plead with them to desist. It is estimated that Western Democracies have spent almost three trillion dollars in foreign aid for Africa since 1960 with little evidence of positive results. Whether one system was worse or better than the other hardly seems to support true PROGRESS, so using that premise as a basis for upper level Social Studies courses is premature at best.

Be that as it may, the most negative aspect of this new amorphous subject has evolved into its insidious opportunity for propaganda and brainwashing. Witness the overwhelming anti-Americanism that has become evident. Many of our graduates openly speak about it now, many even demonstrate against our neighbor who has been protecting us from our enemies ever since our Federal Governmen emasculated our armed forces in 1960's and 1970's. I once asked a Grade Two class which is the worst country in the world. I expected no answer or maybe Russia since we were in the middle of the Cold War. I was dismayed, but enlightened to have an immediate response, " The United States". Was I surprised? Of course, but it showed one how early and thorough this brainwashing had become.

Recently, I received a report about a poster displayed prominently in a Separate (Catholic) Junior High School in Edmonton. I quote the entire letter because it succinctly states the point that I am trying to make:

"Personal propaganda delivered by professors to young adults in colleges and universities is bad enough but, don't be fooled, the same "messages" are being delivered by our grade school teachers. After all, if you want to brainwash someone don't wait until they can judge for themselves.

A school in Edmonton promotes self-loathing among twelve year olds by posting one teacher's personal political biases prominently on its hallway walls in a large poster stating Terrorist R (written backwards to quickly catch the eye of our modern "consumer" children) Us. Its message essentially tells these kids that, because they like fast food and nice clothes, etc., they are responsible for terrorism. Next to it is another poster, showing a large boot kicking the backside of the Americans accompanied by some pretty unflattering language about our freedom-loving neighbors.

When I shared my concerns over these messages with my trustee I was told that these posters supported the District's belief that we must "treat alternative ways of interpreting the world with tolerance and understanding" and that "As a pluralistic society, Canadians embrace multiple points of view". Funny, but those hallway walls were deathly silent when it came to displaying any other point of view." (Sharon Maclise, 2006, Reprinted by permission)

The answer she received begged the question saying this poster was merely a display of our great respect and love for the Freedom of Expression. Really? Where do we find the opposite viewpoint? I can honestly say without reservation, that in my almost 50 years of entering hundreds of schools I have not once found a poster praising Capitalism or the United States, and neither did the author of this letter when she searched several schools after this encounter. Meanwhile, I have been in classrooms where the works of Karl Marx,

Che Guevera, Fidel Castro, Mao Tse Tung, Vladimir Lenin, Kruschev, and Mohatma Ghandi were almost the only ones available, along with posters and charts extolling their accomplishments. Search as I might, not one positive expose of Ronald Reagan, Margaret Thatcher, Golda Meir, Ayn Rand, or Chiang Kai Chek appeared anywhere easily visible. Occasionally, one could find a photo and brief biography of Winston Churchill. What kind of Freedom of Expression is that? Moreover and more important, Junior High students, even Senior High students have so little knowledge of history and life that they have few answers for the sophisticated attack by a teacher or other adult. These kind of propaganda posters should have no place in a school.

Social Studies is also a perfect vehicle for advancing a teacher's or school's pet projects, such as PETA, Greenpeace, Anti-Smoking, World Hunger, Pro-choice, Homophobia, Nuclear Disarmament, the list goes on. (These topics have been covered in Chapter VI so no need to recount them.) Food Banks are common sights in school hallways, and Halloween is touted as a day to ask for donations for UNISEF. If you think these projects aren't going on you haven't been in too many schools or classrooms lately. Teachers are not required by law to answer parents' questions about their support for a political party, philosophical belief, membership in a charitable or benevolent society, membership in an organized religion, or other kind of a belief system. In fact, they are specifically under obligation (possibly with professional penalties if they disobey) to avoid these subjects in the classroom and to refuse to answer these questions from parents and/or guardians. They argue that teachers have the right to personal privacy? I guess our children's minds are not worth considering.

In the upper grades it is forbidden to have debates involving politicians running for office, or preachers, or company representatives, or other adults personally committed to a special way of life in order to present their points of view. As educators we should be advocating and presenting the dialectic in order to teach critical thinking. As well, to allow such debates would be far more honest in demonstrating the principle of freedom of expression in my opinion. It would also serve to teach a valuable lesson in responsible voting for teenagers approaching their age of majority. Rather than simply exhorting citizens to "Go out and vote", we would be teaching them to examine the policies and principles of the various candidates *before* entering the polling booth.

I recall with dismay my first experience with voting, when I was faced with a list of possible candidates with little idea whom I wanted as my choice. I picked one at random, hardly a responsible way to choose. I vowed "Never again." (And I haven't. If I don't have a rational choice, I make sure I go to vote, but leave it blank, a far better choice than choosing at random. People have given their lives for these principles; it is incumbent on us to respect their efforts.) As it stands now, these fundamentals are filtered through the interpretations of a teacher or a school board initiative, or possibly departmental guidelines. The question comes to mind that then how is a parent to judge what general life lessons these teachers and schools are imparting to their children?

Polls have told us that, in the last fifty years, teachers as a group and as within their union organizations have overwhelmingly supported the NDP and, later, the Liberal Party as that Party turned further and further toward government interference in directing our personal lives. The results of those polls definitely point to the general "Leftish" political direction of the professionals who run the institutions which our children MUST attend. In the past, when teachers were busy teaching the more objective subjects of geography and history from textbooks prepared by a panel of writers who were under strict copyright restrictions these trends would not have had such an impact. Even in these textbooks, there still remains huge areas where a specific point of view can be advanced; for example, in the choice of events to be included. For example, those of you older than 50 can recall the study of European history which seemed to include nothing but war after war among various kings and princes. I consider that using those events as demonstrations of the most important historical aspects is another questionable approach to this important study. No wonder many students were turned off by history. However, for those of us who were paying attention, exposure to this history did alert us to the fact that capitalism as opposed to dictatorship in all its many forms, including communism, allowed the general population to enjoy long periods of peace *and prosperity,* in comparison to our "neighbor north of the North Pole", as one of my students humorously explained.

David Horowitz has written a book called *Indoctrination U* exposing the overwhelming number of professors in North American universities who swing leftward in their lectures. Some were openly In retrospect and considering how prevalent a certain educational bias has evolved, the wonder is that there still remains a few graduates of those institutions who have opposing viewpoints.

To "add salt to the wound" another event occurred which has truly made us wonder where this left wind will end. David Suzuki, the high priest of the Global Warming hysteria and supporter of the Kyoto Accord, was in Calgary in late February, 2007. One of his stops was at a public elementary school where he made several disparaging remarks about our Prime Minister, saying in effect, that is was a bad idea to vote for him because of his lack of total acceptance of the Kyoto Accord. There were a few parents at this meeting, who repeated his message outside otherwise who would know? His remarks were heard by all the elementary students in attendance which constitutes direct propaganda, something that is in direct contradiction to the Alberta School Act. For some "unknown" reason the School Board did not censure his remarks.

This example of propagandizing our children was surpassed by yet another egregious factor. Suzuki was in the midst of a cross-country tour in his big motorbus. He would be the first to point out the demerits of using such a bus for any service in light of the need for protecting the environment from greenhouse gases, his own pet project. Using it for a political campaign should be totally unacceptable. It was also reported that the whole entourage was paid for through his charitable organization, the David Suzuki Foundation. Such a designation requires that its sponsors stay far away from any political affiliation if it wishes to retain is non-taxable status. Will this happen? I am not holding my breath. This example just serves to support the argument that some ideas are more acceptable than others. Public education is a wonderful means by which these ideas can be spread.

In Science we encounter somewhat the same problem. This subject was severely watered down in Alberta by instituting Science 10, 20, and 30 as an alternative to the more pure Biology, Chemistry, and Physics prior to the 1990's. Both Science and Mathematics programs have been further democratized supposedly to accommodate non-academic students, so much so that many of the Science 24, Math 14 courses are nothing more than kitchen science or a re-introduction of concepts students should have encountered in elementary school. This example follows the general policy whereby the Spiral Curriculum re-works concepts introduced earlier plus the No-Fail policy as part of the New Directions in Education, discussed in Chapter One. Generally, it panders to the lowest common denominator (student who have little interest in higher education) while the serious scholar becomes more and more turned off. Long term results of this policy can have little but negative effects on our society as a whole.

Another subject that should be given more teaching time during senior science classes is the concept of Evolution. It seems we have almost returned to the philosophical level at the time of the Scopes trial in 1925. While it may be true that Evolution is a hard pill to swallow if you have a belief in Life after Death, that is a question of Faith and should definitely not enter into public education. From my point of view, Evolution is a time and scientifically-tested THEORY, no longer a hypothesis. It is fundamental to the professions of engineering, geology, medicine, pharmacology, architecture, and any profession related to science, in fact, any person who wishes to succeed in our modern interconnected world where events around the world affect us daily. Adults, today, in any of the industrialized world find it increasingly difficult to ignore this science in their everyday lives. We need, at the very least, a general knowledge of evolution and our place on this tree of life. Be that as it may, if parents were permitted to choose the type of education for their children, we could rid ourselves of the vexing problem of whether to learn about evolution or not. It is our right to learn or not as we choose, because those choices will affect us in the future, and therefore we must live with the consequences of our choices. In a public education program all these fundamental questions seem to be decided by bureaucratic decree.

Other subjects such as Literature, Art, and even Mathematics can be skewed to promote values promoted by a public bureaucracy. Examples abound. Math can consist of problems regarding the effects of acid rain while Science can focus on the possible near extinction of various animals. Children read story after story, or view film after film, about our mistreatment of the aboriginals, for example, or our exploitation of colonies. Stories for remedial students seem to consist largely of juvenile delinquents who have turned their lives around, or greedy capitalists who are brought to justice. Professional days often consist of speakers who are "reformed" criminals. In my mind, this does more to glamorize these life choices than teach virtue.

Much of the reason for watering down so many tough subjects is so that students will not suffer feelings of inadequacy. Remember, one must protect and enhance a child's self-esteem at all costs. If a student is expected to experience only success never failure, there is no incentive to DO anything that causes the least bit of discomfort, pain, or exertion. Most of us, after our initial natural instincts to walk and talk have passed, can advance mentally only through deliberate, personal efforts. Success is often elusive, and failure is a great teacher. If everything is "wonderful"," super", "excellent" what incentive is there us to strive harder?

The main public school goal seems to be to attain that coveted Grade 12 Diploma. I believe that one does no favors to a child to cater to mental laziness in favor of being granted a piece of paper called a Diploma. In my books this attitude creates false self-esteem which lasts only until the child leaves the institution. How pathetic it is to encounter a grown man or woman who has been "through" school (as the joke goes, " in one door and out the other") only to discover they lack the academic skills of a normal elementary grade student. That is when one finally understands the true value of a good education ... too late for most of them. Pride has a way of interfering with admitting that you failed to act when you had the chance. How much better it would be to be tested gradually over the years, when your adult guardians and peers had lower expectations of your efforts, and you had the opportunity to learn in a largely safe, non-threatening atmosphere. Life expects great things of us, as we do of ourselves. There is no greater gift we can give our children than to require them to acquire a sound education defined by mastering certain disciplines so that they feel equal to the task

CHAPTER TEN – SAFETY IS KILLING PHYSICAL EXERCISE

"Better Safe than Sorry, or Are We Sorry and Depressed from Being Safe?"
Alar Aksberg, *Yes to Logos*, 2002

The introduction of Physical Education into our schools had a noble objective in the beginning … "Building a sound mind in a sound and active body." The two should go hand in hand. Prior to 1950 little provision had been made for Physical Education programs in most schools except to provide a large open playground with perhaps some goal posts at either end for soccer or football and a net and base outline for a game of softball. The school day was organized to provide a morning and afternoon recess for outdoor play plus leaving a minimum of one hour at noon for both eating lunch and free time. The main job of the teacher was to provide supervision, (which largely consisted of keeping a watchful eye and insisting on universal participation) being the arbiter whenever a dispute arose, or giving assistance whenever someone got hurt.

My early memories for this period consist of a hastily eaten lunch (perhaps ten minutes) and out to play. In retrospect, I recall my teachers getting involved in some supervision, but I was not aware that involving all students in play was a requirement of their jobs. I learned later that if someone was left standing idly by the sidelines it was the teacher's job to take that child by the hand and firmly suggest to a group that "Jenny wants to play, too." As a beginning teacher in the 1960's this became part of my job, too. Running was preferred over walking during these recreational times. Rene Levesque mentions this in his Autobiography relating to his boyhood school experiences prior to World War II. "The

Brothers did not interfere in our games unless they saw someone standing instead of running." (*Rene Levesque on Rene Levesque,* by Rene Levesque, c1980)

Every parent knows that young children have a natural, innate desire to move and be active. Their greater difficulty is to keep the little ones amused and quiet, especially when they are with company. At home the task of providing an outlet for movement and active play was a matter of having some outdoor space, of which there was plenty. Most homes had a good size yard, but playground equipment , if there was any, consisted mainly of swings and teeter-totters. Children longed for a good, large tree which would be sturdy enough to support a swing made from a rope with a piece of plank for a seat. Generally, children made up their own fun, playing Hide and Seek, Pum Pum Pullaway, Ante, Ante, I Over, Prisoners' Base, and a myriad of other similar games needing little or no equipment and much running.

In our large family the biggest obstacle to our bursting into activity was to find the time to do it. Everyone over the age of five or six had chores and duties to perform. Much the same situation existed in other families. To be fair, physical activity during school hours for girls declined as they got older and especially during the winter. By High School girls stood and chatted for the most part during breaks; the boys practiced throwing a baseball or football. However, we must not forget that children walked to and from school, distances of up to three miles each way. So physical activity was taken care of by these two aspects, namely, home chores and a great deal of walking during the day.

As farms became larger during the 1960s and 1970s many of the local country schools were closed making it necessary to institute bussing of students. How fortunate it seemed for my younger brother and sisters! Few people worried about the resulting elimination of the healthful walks to and from school.

Soon, however, the need for a physical activity program during the school day was raised as a school necessity. The question arose as to how could one prepare and execute a good Physical Education program for the schools without the necessary prerequisites, including gymnasia, equipment, and personnel. The cry for this program emanated from the universities and the Departments of Education. School Boards felt the pressure, but lacked the funds for these expensive buildings, equipment, and staff. It was then that provincial governments became involved, enacting the laws to make Physical Education a compulsory subject, and providing some of the funds. School Boards subsequently, found themselves in the unenviable position of finding dollars for this new directive. School taxes needed to be substantially increased.

By 1975, in our travels between Victoria, British Columbia, and Norquay, Saskatchewan (with a couple of stops in between) every school we encountered had acquired these necessities. Now we could all heave a sigh of relief. Good physical growth and development would automatically follow. Right? Not exactly, as time would tell.

During my entire years of schooling, neither myself nor any of my contemporaries in country schools possessed a gymnasium, indoor facilities, or a special teacher for physical activity yet we attained generally much healthier and fitter bodies than in today's population of the same age. Polls by Statistics Canada attest to this fact. Obesity was a problem for only a small minority of adults, and an extreme rarity among children. Fancy running shoes, helmets, and protective gear of all kinds were almost unheard of. Accidents happened, but with the resilience of youth, we dusted ourselves off, the teacher applied iodine and a simple bandage and we went back to our running game.

Mistakes made during this introductory stage were to be expected. Some of the activities chosen were totally inappropriate. As a Physical Education teacher during the 1960s I was involved in teaching gymnastics as part of the curriculum. This activity produced great danger for students. Older girls, especially, did not welcome this activity, and with good reason. They could and did get serious injuries. I have adjusted my dedication to this activity considerably since then. While simple tumbling was okay for the younger ones, using olympic equipment must be left to professional trainers. Trampolines had just appeared and became a fad proliferating like the proverbial mushrooms. It soon became apparent that jumping on a trampoline could result in horrendous accidents. I recall a few of them during my school career that still make me cringe. I shall not recount them. Certainly, these two activities should best be done under the supervision of an expert.

Over the years physical activities in school have undergone huge changes. Safety and security have become major concerns. The inevitable accidents have resulted in court cases where judges found schools and their personnel lacking. Next followed laws, rules, regulations, and restrictions as to what could be done to prevent these accidents in the name of Safety. Who could ague with Safety? It was a sacred trust. Now we can examine the results from the perspective of 30+ years and the picture is not that great.

Overall, many of these new safety measures led to very negative results in terms of physical fitness. In fact, physical fitness and obesity have become major health concerns among the youth as well as for the young adult population, most of whom have experienced this enlightened physical education program. It is time to re-evaluate what we are doing and decide how to best improve the abysmal results.

An article in the *Edmonton Journal* (also making the rounds on the email sites, no author) stated,

> "According to today's regulators and bureaucrats, those of us who were kids in the '30s, 40s, 50s, 60s, 70s, and even early 80s, probably shouldn't have survived. Our baby cribs were covered with bright lead-based paints. We had no childproof lids on medicine bottles, doors or cabinets and when we rode our bikes, we had no helmets.

... We drank water from a garden hose and not from a bottle. Horrors! ... We would leave home in the morning and play all day as long as we were back when the street lights came on. No one was able to reach us all day. No cell phones. Unthinkable! Yet "This generation has produced some of the best risk-takers, problem-solvers, and inventors ever. " (*Edmonton Journal, Insert,* September 20, 2004)

Mark Steyn wrote an article that same year denouncing Ontario legislature for implementing compulsory bike helmets for adults (compulsory use of helmets for children had been law for some time already) saying, " So the question is whether, among the 70 or 80 cycling fatalities each year, the small number (if any) of lives saved by wearing helmets outweighs the social costs of discouraging what was hitherto an agreeable form of exercise. " He called this type of interfering in the freedom of choice we should be exercising as families and adults "... a cotton-candy cocoon of illusory security binding its subjects ever tighter." (Mark Steyn, *Western Standard,* December 6, 2004) I love his choice of words.

The argument that accidents cost the public health system more money is specious at best. " That's actually an argument not against cycling, but against government health care." (Mark Steyn, *Western Standard,* December 6, 2004) I couldn't agree more.

Some of the new measures that have been implemented in schools which have impacted negatively on physical fitness and activities within the last twenty years are as follows:

1. Recesses for elementary grades have been cut from two (morning & afternoon) to one only in the morning. In one Texas school recesses were cancelled altogether in order to curb widespread bullying and violence. (*ATA News,* January 28, 2003) It is not uncommon for schools with Grades 1 to 6 dividing the recess into time for Grades 1 to 3, another time for Grades 4 to 6 for safety reasons.
2. Children ride buses if they are more than ten blocks away and to various activities even if distances are within reasonable walking distances.

3. Recesses are cancelled if the weather is minus 25 degrees Celsius, in spite of the fact that today's winter clothing is much better and more easily obtained than in the past. I don't remember ever being kept inside because of weather as a school child, perhaps during a severe blizzard.

4. Noon hours are now called Lunch "Breaks" and last for 35 to 45 minutes as a general rule; the children are dismissed after first having lunch. Rarely does this Break allow children to play more than one-half hour. Many of these Lunch Breaks are taken up by special activities, such as choir or student meetings.

5. Many outdoor field trips have been cancelled due to safety concerns.

6. One school refused to allow students to be billeted or to ride in parents' vehicles due to safety and insurance concerns. This rule must apply to all the other schools in this district.

7. Insurance costs have gone through the roof due to judges' decisions regarding School Board and teacher liability in cases of accidents.

8. The paperwork on field trips has become overwhelming for many teachers and coaches because of safety rules and regulations. Only really determined teachers carry it through, then generally avoid the whole hassle the next time round.

9. Interschool sports has been severely restricted due to extra costs such as the necessity of using licensed drivers and public vehicles rather than private automobiles as well as using parents as billeting partners. (How different from my experience when I was a Phys. Ed. Teacher the 1960's when I piled six students into my Volkswagon to transport them to a neighboring school for a game of volleyball.)

10. Playground equipment now must meet such stringent requirements that few can afford them without massive fund-raising.

11. Much of the new playground equipment that meets safety standards, such as the new teeter-totters, is so "safe" to use that it holds fascination only for the very young.

12. Children must wear a helmet if they are cycling. This law applies to any child who is riding even a tricycle. This is the law, and parents or school personnel who do not insist on helmets can face severe penalties. An entire lobby group has emerged wanting to force EVERYONE to obey this restriction. Polls show the number of people riding bicycles has dropped significantly.

13. Authorities have warned people to stay out of the sun when it becomes high overhead, wear protective clothing or use a high number sunscreen. Schools generally avoid letting students be in the sun for any length of time. Evidence is emerging that the sun is good for you and has great healthful powers.

Taken one at a time these rules and regulations seem to be very sane and sensible, but multiply one on top of another, and they become draconian. Safety First has become Safety First, Second, Third and …. ? Let's get back to some sense of moderation and sanity.

I see trampolines again becoming a home appliance, and I view them with apprehension. It is good to observe that most of them have safety nets and covered springs. Most schools avoid them, and parents are wise to hesitate unless and until they get proper instruction and training. All in all, certain physical activities are too dangerous for the average person and should not be included in a school program. However, the fact that an accident has occurred should not be sufficient reason for any physical activity to be removed completely or so tied up in paperwork and insurance concerns that most teachers, and consequently their students, avoid getting involved. We should get rid of the philosophy that "If it saves the life on one child no cost is too great." My response for that extreme statement is to ask, "What about the fact that it saves one child's life, but makes five million children miserable and impairs their health for a lifetime? Is that worth it?"

Another unfortunate corollary to our government-mandated, more sedentary life-style is the heavy emphasis on organized sports and activities for children. "Go outside and play." was a standard command from myself and most mothers and teachers prior to 1980. Few adults were involved in what that play would entail. Kids were trusted to figure out the details.

Conditions have changed significantly in the last quarter century. The Canadian Council on Learning found that in 2003 31% of children's free time was committed to structured, organized and supervised activities. They also reported in 2006 that unstructured play has many more benefits than just keeping the kids from underfoot so adults can attend to their own affairs. Previously, children used their imaginations and powers of negotiation to decide among themselves what games they should play, what the rules should be, and even what the penalties should be for non-compliance. If you took your ball and went home in anger, your punishment would be to play alone; a condition which generally exacted enough of a penalty to discourage the petulant one from doing it again. It was not unusual to witness bribery as the way to negotiate oneself back into the game.

It is well-known that children need to run off excess energy in order to focus their minds later on more academic pursuits. All of these mental and emotional decisions allow youngsters to develop important life skills as well as to study better. Whatever the benefits of organized activities, and they are many, they limit children's abilities to develop their cooperative skills among their peers, one of the important life skills. This applies on the schoolyard as well, with teachers and supervisors there to encourage active play rather than allowing children to sit in corners admiring the newest toy brought in by the kid with the biggest budget. This fact encompasses my objection to swim classes DURING SCHOOL TIME. It not only interferes with academic learning but also time for free play.

Furthermore, extra classes in specialized activities means a great deal of time and money spent needlessly on travel arrangements.

It seems I am not the only one crying in the wilderness. Here are just a few of the articles written on this subject:

- "Just let the kids go out and play" (Naomi Lakritz, *Calgary Herald,* April 5, 2007);
- "Running and yelling is good for you" (Donna Swimiarski, *ATA News,* January 28, 2003);
- "The civilizing wilderness. A B.C. teacher says hiking is good for obesity and lack of discipline that ails modern students." (Candis McLean, *The Report,* October 7, 2002);
- "Not enough street hockey" (Candis McLean, *Alberta Report,* February 8, 1998);
- "Olympian says, the solution to childhood obesity is simple: PLAY!" (Valerie Berenyi, *Calgary Herald,* April 24, 2006);
- "Change urged in way kids play." (*Calgary Herald,* September 11, 2007);
- I quote from the last one: "270 professionals blame 'the marked deterioration in children's mental health on an overprotective society and too much sedentary entertainment.."

Why aren't our politicians listening?

An innovative program at the University of Alberta has recently come to my attention. Several Summer Camps for children have mixed both physical training and mental concentration in their programs on the basis that the mind works better after exercise. Research had shown that many associations seriously interested in physical fitness also found that attaining fitness also increased their mental functioning. For example, the Roman Legions began their days by skipping rope. "Movement adds Oxygen to our blood, balances our action hormones and increases mental awareness." (www.FattoFit in

Minutes.com, 2007) Why are our schools refusing to acknowledge the necessity of exercise, especially for young children?

Restrictions on physical activity has resulted in our young people doing less and less physical activity during school hours. Recent studies point to the lack of exercise as the major cause of childhood obesity, not fast food as was originally surmised. Obesity has, in turn, resulted in increased levels of childhood diabetes, and possibly even asthma and allergic reactions. Consequently, many (polls suggest up to 25%) are suffering severe health problems which often continue into adulthood and last for their entire lives.

I lay the blame for these overly protective laws and institutions purely at the feet of governments and their appointees, since that is where the problem originated. Only governments have the power to bring some sanity to this area of concern. Safety rules and guidelines should be tested for common sense and be up to the general discretion of the supervisor. There must be strict limits on the financial liability of the instructor or the school unless there is evidence of easily avoidable malfeasance. Actually, a great deal of the extra costs have been forced on the schools by the unions, so limiting the authority of top-heavy unions should help to solve some of these problems. Above all, we must recognize that accidents will happen, and one tragedy should not prevent whole generations from enjoying the great adrenaline rush of physical achievement, competition, and the good health, both physical and mental, that follows.

EPILOGUE & CONCLUSION

"A civilization is not conquered by the powers without, so much as by the rot within."

William Durant , c1940

What does all this discussion and disclosure add up to? You may well ask. I have come to believe that compulsory public education should be disbanded. Parents, families, teachers, and their customers, the children, should decide whether and when they should go to school, or whether they want to learn on their own, by sailing around the world for example. (Certainly we have read or heard of such strange occurrences.) Furthermore, these same parties should pay for this precious commodity, or accept the benevolence of others who are concerned and offer to provide for it. Every day we hear of people such as Oprah Winfrey or various Church and Non-Government Societies that roam the world searching for just such a need. Personally, I have two friends who have made this quest a special part of their retirement. Good on them, I say. I strongly suspect that people such as they are the honest educators in the true sense of the word. More important still, this solution returns the honor and respect due to parents for the decisions about educating their own children.

And what of the teachers? What is their role? Under this system they would have two basic choices, as have all other professionals; that is, join a school already set up and adhering to your own personal goals , or start a school of your own. I daresay there would appear many small "Daycare Schools" in a community for the little ones, especially. Think of the problems that would solve. No more long bus rides. Fewer problems with bigger kids bullying or teasing as happens in a large institution. Everyone knows everyone else by name (and probably house number). Children could come home for lunch, stay and eat lunch there, or have it provided by some local business, maybe a stay-at-home parent, who welcomes the opportunity to get out of the house for awhile, besides making a few dollars for her/his efforts. You can be sure there would be no extra costs associated. Lots of parental involvement would be easily implemented, if desired, without going through extensive security checks. It would be difficult if not impossible for a pedophile to hide from a group of gossipy (or should I say, talkative) parents.

In the upper grades parents could become important contributors to studies and information about their outside professions and trades rather than just sources of financial contributions. I know that one reason I stayed away from many Parent-School meetings was to avoid the constant demands on our family income. Time was a precious commodity as well, and who wants and loves to go to meetings? It seemed that whenever I did go it turned into a planning session for a teacher-appreciation event, or a discussion on what should be the next fund-raiser. Rarely, if ever, did we get to discuss the subject matter or management procedures being offered and used by the school. I know *I* was turned off.

However, we did go to every Parent-Teacher interview offered, as I urge every parent to do likewise. This practice makes an important statement on behalf of your child. "Yes, Sir, or Ma'am, I care very much about what's happening in school and in the classroom." " I do NOT expect you to give my daughter/son extra special attention, but I DO expect you to answer his/her questions every day as long as they are not merely being cheeky and/or disrespectful.' (One teacher whose policy I admire offered each child the opportunity to ask one short question per class. That practice seems fair and balanced to me.) 'And I DO expect you to give me an thorough and honest assessment of their educational progress." "I will NOT be satisfied with a vague, emotional response, like 'Your Johnny is so-o polite and I love him to be in my classroom.'" What does that mean? It appears to put the teacher's needs first while my child is just an accessory to that need.

If education was not compulsory, teenage students would be able to leave and get involved in something more productive as soon as they became bored/disinterested/turned-off by school. Nothing teaches better than Life Experience about the important things, so why not get on with it. In our highly artificial, modern society where children are coddled and protected from most things natural, these life experiences become even more critical. Add to this the hundreds of opportunities there are to continue to learn throughout life, the main wonder is why we insist on sticking to an old model, long outdated.

It was interesting to hear a commentary on Shaw Cable that there was a serious lack of skilled tradesmen in Western Canada at present, due in large part to the general emphasis on encouraging students to seek the professions rather than training for the trades during their school years. Indeed, this same statement could be said for conditions across Canada. Why didn't the government foresee such needs and plan for it? I say give parents in consultation with their children control of their education and curtail government interference in this area, and the families affected could react more quickly to new conditions. They, the parents and children, could certainly not do a worse job of planning for the future than governments have done in the past.

Regulations insisting that children attend school until they are 15 or 16 (as in Alberta today) does nothing good for education. I am not sure whether children need merely 100 hours to learn the Basics, as John Gatto surmised, but I am certain these skills don't require 10 or 12 years. Warming a seat in school is not only unproductive, but has contributed to the great increase in disrespect for most adults and their values along with the rising dangers associated with going to school. It only makes them resent school, their teachers, and finally any and all authorities, at least for many of their adolescent years. This has led to school becoming a glorified baby sitting service, which it definitely should not be.

Young men, in particular those with little interest in book learning, would be much better served by getting involved in apprenticeship programs such as motor and vehicle mechanics, construction, and the thousand and one trades and businesses that require hands-on learning. There are many practical, apprenticeship careers for girls as well. It is time we stopped treating our young people like babies and send them out into the real world when they show little interest in schooling. Years ago a child was considered to be an adult at 13 years old. Maybe our grandparents had tuned into the *real* rhythms of nature.

Attempting not to end on a negative note I will now mention some of the positive things that have occurred in Education since World War II (which is the main focus of this book).

An outstanding example of success that comes to mind is the establishment of language immersion schools. The impetus for this step forward resulted as an offshoot of the Bilingual and Bicultural Act of 1968, after pressure from Quebec. The people of that province, namely the French-speaking ones realized that the French language was fast becoming a minority language and in danger of disappearing completely from the North American scene. Therefore they pressured Prime Minister Pierre Trudeau, one of their own French Canadians from Quebec, to enact equal status with English for the French language throughout the Rest of Canada. This Act has resulted in enormous sums of money being spent on all government documents in both languages and sent to all parts of Canada. Many of these documents remained unused and ended up in landfills, a very negative result of that action. However, for the enlightenment of the mind there has been a few surprising benefits for English-speaking Canadians.

The first bilingual French immersion school was started in Calgary in 1974. My sister's oldest son was enrolled in that school, as have been her other son, my son and several of the children and now grandchildren of my immediate family. For myself, I had taken the old grammar French since Grade Nine and supplemented it with numerous adult classes in French plus additional classes in Russian, Spanish, Italian, and Ukrainian throughout my life. These classes and language tapes, etc. have been very helpful when traveling to various countries, but fall far short of knowing a language fluently. They also were started much too late. It is now known that a child can learn a language by eidetic memory up to the age of twelve or thereabouts. After that age, language learning must take place by a process of association and memorization, which is far less thorough. More than that, pronunciation becomes difficult at best. Mouth, lips, tongue and facial muscles required to pronounce certain sounds are developed early. When language learning is delayed it often means the student simply cannot pronounce certain sounds correctly, if at all.

Multiple language learning has been very helpful in more ways than just being able to speak another language. Studies show that knowledge of a second or third language develops parts of the brain that no other learning can accomplish. Furthermore, knowing another language well contributes much to a person's true self-confidence especially for those of us who like to travel, meaning most of the population of the affluent Western democracies. It was very revealing to me when crossing the border into northern Quebec and suddenly being faced with business people and others who spoke no English. The same thing happened when traveling in Europe where many of the citizens are multilingual. Suddenly, talkative and happy people became very quiet and withdrawn, their self-image taking a serious blow. This realization becomes compounded when confronted with others who can speak English as well as chatter away in another language. "Are they talking about me? I wonder what they are saying? " Suddenly you are in another dimension.

Although Canada has been and continues to be a country of immigrants from all parts of the world, the use of languages other than English (or French in Quebec) was discouraged and, in fact, regarded as demeaning. So most of those of us born in Canada after 1930 became largely unilingual, a most unfortunate circumstance in my opinion. Many of the people with whom I went to school or worked with over the years were blessed with the ability to speak another language and could have conducted lessons or conversation sessions in these language, but were marginalized on that prejudicial basis, i.e. that English and French were the only acceptable languages to learn. For example, the school system mandated that everyone must take French lessons starting in Grade 9, as I stated earlier. Meanwhile in the area of Saskatchewan where I lived there were very few French speaking people, maybe one or two families, whereas there were many families who spoke Ukrainian, Russian, German, Swedish, and Norwegian in our little corner of the country. Yet here we were taking French from a unilingual English teacher, while another precious resource, people with other First Languages, were disregarded and their language-speaking ability discouraged to the extent many of us with access to a second language at home refused to speak or learn it.

Over the years, the introduction of French Immersion programs has proliferated throughout Western Canada, fully funded by the Departments of Education. There still remains the problem of accessibility, however. I still recall standing in line for two hours early one chilly May morning to try to enroll my daughter in a Late Immersion French program only to get to the front and find out she was the sixty-third enrollee with a cut-off at sixty maximum. The only way she could enter was if three others were to drop out before September. This never happened so she continued to take the regular French as a Second Language program which she had been doing since Grade 3. Interestingly enough, that program (which was considered superior to the old Grammar) program proved to be as inadequate as the former. In order to learn another language, one needs early immersion, that is hearing and speaking only the new language for an extended period of time, not intermittently and with explanations in English.

It was a pity that no languages other than French had been offered in the public schools as part of the publicly funded curriculum until recently. Different ethnic groups had organized Saturday classes or after-school programs to facilitate the continuance of their language, but all planning, management, and financing remained their own responsibility. I am not against parents paying for learning another language, just that it is unfair when this program is offered to some students and not to others.

At present, I am happy to report, things have improved even more in this area. French is not the only language being offered by many schools. Spanish bilingual schools are becoming common, as are German, Russian, and lately languages such as Mandarin, then Arabic since 9/11. It has become recognized that learning a language brings with it appreciation of cultural differences and contributions as well as the ability to communicate in another language . If there is a downside, it might be that some cultural groups are becoming so introspective that they don't see the need to learn English at all, but that is another story.

Another positive development in recent years has been the introduction of Charter Schools in Alberta. Moreover, the government has seen fit to implement a policy (at least partially) to fund some private schools. This not only means parents have more control of their children's education, but also puts some pressure on the Public Schools to become more responsive to parents' and individuals' wishes. I contend that this could be the main reason for Alberta having demonstrated the best results across Canada in literacy tests in recent years. (Statistics Canada, 2005) I also understand some high schools are offering classes in trades where students study for part of the time, then pair up with a business to do apprenticeship on-the-job training at the job-site. Excellent idea, but why does it cost taxpayer dollars? It sounds as though this training can have monitory advantages for the business as well as the student, and should be cost-neutral.

Hundreds of studies have been done on the effectiveness of various curricula and methodologies, but the findings of these studies have been largely ignored by the official spokespeople for education. Educators should study these results resolutely with open minds, not cling stubbornly to outmoded ideas. For example, the goal of Self-Esteem became such a sacred cow that teachers were even allowed to "fudge" student marks so as not to damage a child's self-esteem. Horrors! This meant that a teacher should change the final mark to a passing grade. It was justified because so many of the students were failing. There is no need for me to tell you how bad this policy was for the unfortunate students affected, in their future life. The bureaucrats didn't seem to care. It was a way to avoid an immediate problem.

I was sent an interesting email the other day claiming that Prohibition in the United States was not abolished (1920-1934) because of the rise in crime and corruption that it produced, but merely because the government needed more revenues and realized they could get it from alcohol. In other words, it wasn't Common Sense that dictated a change in policy for the better, but a pecuniary need. It seems Governments are the last ones to give way to Reason when certain policies are clearly wrong-headed. It will require a great outcry from citizens to make a dint in the walls of resistant built around this seemingly impregnable fortress.

Public pressure seems to be the only method available to the ordinary citizen. You can exercise this pressure through expressing your views on education and by your vote in elections. Obstacles abound. Statistics show that only about 35% of eligible voters participate in municipal elections where school board members are selected. I am not surprised at the low turnout. It is very difficult to get information on where the various candidates stand, even for someone like myself who is vitally interested. My daughter tried to find information by going through the internet, but not all candidates have the time, money, or expertise to develop a website. None of their expenses are tax-deductible, neither are cash donations from others, as I found out myself in 1992. It almost seems like a conspiracy to maintain the system as it stands. I urge you to make your voices heard by whatever means available.

Certainly a better, more positive, intermediary step to improving Education would be to bring in Voucher Education where the tax dollar follows the child to whichever school the parent wishes. Thus, results could show whether less involvement is a better move for the future.

My best judgment suggests that Departments of Education should be shrunk to the dimensions of supplying a minimal curriculum for various levels, certifying teachers, plus developing, administering, and grading standardized tests. Then – hands off! Let parents (then students themselves as they get older) decide which schools they want to attend, what additional courses they wish to take, and then PAY FOR IT themselves. Dan Smoot stated back in 1970 "If the billions now confiscated in taxes for our monstrously expensive government schools were left in the hands of people, there would be enough money in every community to provide real education for children." (*Dan Smoot Report, 1970*) Since his prophetic words costs for public education in both our "freedom-loving societies" have skyrocketed. Through granting liberty of education we truly would encourage diversity and, I believe, the challenge for our progeny to use their minds to the fullest possible extent. Maybe then, Hilda Neatby would rest easy in her grave.

The End

(or maybe the Beginning of Something Better)